Finding Solace
in the Soil

Finding Solace in the Soil

*An Archaeology of Gardens
and Gardeners at Amache*

Bonnie J. Clark

UNIVERSITY PRESS OF COLORADO
Louisville

© 2020 by University Press of Colorado

Published by University Press of Colorado
245 Century Circle, Suite 202
Louisville, Colorado 80027

 The University Press of Colorado is a proud member of
the Association of University Presses.

The University Press of Colorado is a cooperative publishing enterprise supported, in part, by Adams State University, Colorado State University, Fort Lewis College, Metropolitan State University of Denver, Regis University, University of Alaska, University of Colorado, University of Denver, University of Northern Colorado, University of Wyoming, Utah State University, and Western Colorado University.

∞ This paper meets the requirements of the ANSI/NISO Z39.48–1992 (Permanence of Paper)

ISBN: 978-1-64642-092-6 (hardcover)
ISBN: 978-1-64642-337-8 (paperback)
ISBN: 978-1-64642-093-3 (ebook)
https://doi.org/10.5876/9781646420933

Library of Congress Cataloging-in-Publication Data

Names: Clark, Bonnie J., author.
Title: Finding solace in the soil : an archaeology of gardens and gardeners at Amache / Bonnie J. Clark.
Description: Louisville : University Press of Colorado, [2020] | Includes bibliographical references and index.
Identifiers: LCCN 2020028091 (print) | LCCN 2020028092 (ebook) | ISBN 9781646420926 (cloth) | ISBN 9781646423378 (paperback) | ISBN 9781646420933 (ebook)
Subjects: LCSH: Granada Relocation Center. | Garden archaeology—Colorado—Amache. | Excavations (Archaeology)—Colorado—Amache. | Ethnoarchaeology—Colorado—Amache. | Japanese Americans—Colorado—Amache—Antiquities. | Japanese Americans—Colorado—Amache—History. | Japanese Americans—Colorado—Amache—Social life and customs. | Japanese Americans—Evacuation and relocation, 1942-1945.
Classification: LCC SB469.75 .C535 2020 (print) | LCC SB469.75 (ebook) | DDC 635.09788/98—dc23
LC record available at https://lccn.loc.gov/2020028091
LC ebook record available at https://lccn.loc.gov/2020028092

Cover photograph: Mataji Umeda in his garden, courtesy Helen Yagi Sekikawa.

Contents

Figures and Tables

Figures

Tables

Acknowledgments

Like a garden, an archaeological project is nurtured by complicated interdependencies. This book would not exist without the generous spirit of many who unwillingly spent part of their life at Amache but who willingly shared their memories of that time. I am particularly grateful to Minoru Tonai and Carlene Tanigoshi Tinker, both of whom have spent hours talking to me about life in the camp and both of whom provided comments and edits on the draft of this manuscript. Mr. Tonai also connected me to many of the other former incarcerees whose histories are featured in this work, including George Hirano, Thomas Shigekuni, Fumiye Nishizaki, and Alice Fukuda Tanaka. This book is much enriched by my conversations with them, as well as by photographs they and others, especially Jack Muro and Helen Yagi Sekikawa, shared with me. Dennis Fujita and Greg Kitajima also gave me feedback on the book manuscript, while Gary Ono helped me secure the proper rights to Jack Muro's photographs.

Each of the graduate students who served as University of Denver (DU) Amache crew chiefs directed work onsite and at the Amache Museum. This book would not exist without their commitment to community-engaged research. They have been (in year order): April Kamp-Whittaker and Dana Ogo Shew (2008); David Garrison, Kellen Hinrichsen, and Paul Swader (2010); Christian Driver, Jennifer Moon, Peter Quantock, and Natalie Ruhe (2012); Jeremy Haas, April Kamp-Whittaker, Angela Rueda, and Zachary Starke (2014); Rebecca Cruz, Annie Danis, Maeve Herrick, April Kamp-Whittaker, and Sabreina Slaughter (2016); and Cameron Benton, Annie Danis, April Kamp-Whittaker, and Whitney Peterson (2018). The many crew members they oversaw were likewise dedicated to the work at Amache, and I hope each of them sees the fruits of their labor here. I want to particularly thank the former incarcerees who returned to Amache as volunteers on the crew, especially Anita Miyamoto Miller and Carlene Tanigoshi Tinker, who have participated for an astonishing five summers (along with Anita's husband, Duncan Kelly), and Gary Ono and Dennis Fujita, who have both volunteered twice and have been involved in the project in many other ways. Other multiple-year volunteers include Amache descendants Greg Kitajima, Kirsten Leong, and Salvador Valdez-Ono. I am grateful to all of them and to our other community volunteers: Dante Hilton-Ono, Bill and Michael Sueoka, Adam Fujita, Diane Honda, Tyler Nakaue, Howard Ono, Diane Pierce, Arlene Makita-Acuna, Edie Frederick, and Ken Kitajima.

It takes a lot of groceries (also tanks of gas, miles of flagging tape, the list goes on) to support these crews, and I am thankful to the many individuals and organizations that over the years have contributed financially to the DU Amache Project. From the first field season onward, the Japanese Association of Colorado—now the Nikkeijin Kai of Colorado—has financially supported graduate student research at Amache. Its vote of confidence helped set up the project for success. Primary financial support has come from the State Historical Fund of History Colorado and the University of Denver, especially through the Center for Community Engagement to Advance Scholarship and Learning. Other grants that have supported this work have come from the National Park Service and Dumbarton Oaks. A hearty thank you to them and to our individual donors for their support, especially Douglas and Sandra Tashiro and the family of Robert Horiuchi.

The Mile High (Denver) Chapter of the Japanese American Citizens League (JACL) also contributed to project success from the outset by helping us connect to Colorado's Japanese American community. Other chapters of the JACL have kindly helped us reach their members and have often incorporated us into their programming. The national JACL organization has provided support by publishing about the project in its newspaper, the *Pacific Citizen*, and through grants to support the DU Amache traveling exhibit and public presentations about the archaeology of Amache.

As readers will see, this work owes a great deal to people with expertise relevant to the archaeological study of gardens. Steve Archer has served as much more than the project archaeobotanist, and I rely on his level-headed advice both in and out of the field. Erika Marín-Spiotta has guided the study of the site's soil chemistry and, along with Emily Eggleston, set up the protocols we still follow. John G. Jones knows more about archaeological pollen and phytoliths than I can dream of, and I appreciate all his years of research. Jim Casey came onboard in 2010 as a graduate student to help with digital mapping. He has become a valued collaborator, and his efforts to create a high-resolution digital record of the site using drone photography can be seen in the pages to come. Dana Ogo Shew was once my advisee and has continued to contribute to the Amache Project, especially through her expertise in oral history. Finally, April Kamp-Whittaker has been involved in all but two of the six Amache field seasons covered by this book. She is now the project's co-field director, and among her many contributions to project success has been her management of digital resources.

My colleagues at the University of Denver have supported this project in multiple ways, whether through lively discussion, sharing resources, or managing payroll. Many of them have contributed actively by training crews and shaping field protocols. By helping me understand ground-penetrating radar, donating his time and equipment, and overseeing graduate student investigations, Larry Conyers is key to the successful study of Amache's gardens. Since 2012, Anne Amati has served as the museum coordinator for the project, and I rely on her calm wisdom. Christina Kreps, Brooke Rohde, and Esteban Gómez have each consulted on the project and traveled to Amache to work with the crews. The administrative staff of the Department of Anthropology and other divisions have kept the trains running, and I am thankful to all of them, especially Jennifer Foxcroft, Orla McInerney, and Megan Whitman.

I would like to thank Hilary Blair, who consulted with me early on in this project, and everyone at the University Press of Colorado, especially Darrin

Pratt and Charlotte Steinhardt. Finally, Kathleen Corbett has put up with Amache absorbing much of my time and attention for over a decade. If that weren't enough, she spent countless hours editing this manuscript. Thank you for all the ways you have helped this work bloom.

Finding Solace
in the Soil

Prologue

A Visit to Amache

Between the autumn of 1942 and 1945, the High Plains was home to what one wartime newspaper article dubbed "The Strangest City in Colorado" (Casey 1942). If you could go back in time, you'd likely travel there by train, following the ribbon of trees that mark the location of the Arkansas River through otherwise open prairie. Disembarking at the small farming and market town of Granada, a truck from the camp might pick you up for the mile-and-a-half drive south to Amache. During the short journey, you would notice Japanese Americans working in the fields, farming crops to support the thousands of people confined at the War Relocation Authority (WRA) center. Getting closer, you cannot ignore the octagonal guard towers and the barbed wire fences enclosing the core of the camp. After you pass through the fence to a sentry gate, an armed Military Police guard processes you. They might check to make sure you brought no contraband items, such as firearms, alcoholic beverages or, through most of 1942, cameras.

As you move south and uphill through the camp, the administrative area is on your right. The white painted buildings, sidewalks, manicured lawns,

DOI: 10.5876/9781646420933.c000

and young trees create a uniform landscape, like that found in a freshly built industrial park. To your left sits the motor pool, with trucks and jeeps for the MPs. Soon you pass into the area of camp that houses incarcerees. The drab tarpaper-clad buildings go by in waves. However, something else in those blocks would grab your attention—splashes of color and shape from the hundreds of gardens framing the barracks. Some are merely fenced areas with a few flowers or trees encircled in rock. Although small, they might remind you of a typical American front yard. Others, however, stand out as distinctly Japanese, with miniaturized landscapes and ponds or carefully graveled spaces with larger "stones" that on closer inspection are pieces of concrete.

In some blocks, you might notice a group of kids playing marbles or elders with their *Go* boards. They sit underneath shade trees planted alongside common buildings. In other blocks, you see formal garden beds, playgrounds, or baseball backstops in the open areas between buildings. Sometime in the evening, the strains of a swing tune waft from where teenagers or young adults play music. It might be from a record player or a live band set up in a mess hall decorated with colorful crepe paper for a night of dancing.

If an honored guest, you visit Block 6H, the location of the block manager's office. It is that block's recreation hall, but with a sign above the door that says "Amache Town Hall." There you pose for a photograph in the hill-and-pond garden carefully constructed by incarcerees as a showpiece. A resident of the block might recall how the builders unloaded trucks full of rounded river cobble gathered from the banks of the nearby Arkansas River. They point out how cobble encircles the kidney-shaped pond and makes up much of the hill beside it. The chirping coming from the scrap wood birdhouses highlights life in this bright spot so different from the plains that surround it.

If you arrive in the fall, you can join others in visiting the agricultural fair, where individuals, blocks, and school classes show off the best of the produce they grew that season in their victory gardens. Perhaps you'll help judge the displays of *ikebana*, flower arrangements of plants grown at Amache. If you arrived in a different season, you still might be able to see the talents of incarcerees on display in barracks or mess halls. It might strike you how much of the art employs local natural materials like the sand of miniature landscapes, carvings in soft cottonwood, or vases made from the roots of yucca.

However, if you were a visitor of Japanese ancestry, the weight of institutional confinement would soon bear down on you. Although shaded by trees during your wait, you would line up with the others to stream into the mess hall for each meal. At night, you'd stay in a claustrophobic room no more than 20 feet by 24 feet. If your hosts are handy, you can sleep on a bedframe made of scrap lumber or packing crates; otherwise, you rest on the army cot provided by the authorities. There is no plumbing in your room, so if you need the bathroom at night, you head outside to the latrine building. The normally lovely gardens take on an ominous tone when illuminated by a light from the guard tower because it means an MP tracks your nighttime movements. For all the beauty the incarcerees could create, the fact is inescapable: you are in a prison.

1

Introduction

During public presentations about the gardens at Amache, Colorado's World War II Japanese American confinement camp, I am often asked how people incarcerated there accessed plant materials. The pages to come suggest many answers to that question, but one of them is contained in a jar recovered from the site in 2008. That was the first summer of the University of Denver's biannual archaeology and museum field school. The participants were a diverse crew: a former Amache incarceree and his grandson, volunteers from the local high school, undergraduate and graduate students, and professionals like me, a professor of anthropology. We represented the most important stakeholders for this project: those with a personal or family tie to the site, local residents who know the region and are the site stewards, students learning how to study the tangible past, and scholars gathering data for their research. Both onsite and in the museum, we each had something to gain, and working together meant drawing from everyone's skills and commitments.

Two dedicated graduate students, April Kamp-Whittaker and Dana Ogo Shew, were pursuing thesis research at Amache while overseeing the museum

DOI: 10.5876/9781646420933.c001

FIGURE 1.1. Jar of saved seeds collected at Amache, 2008. *Courtesy*, DU Amache Project.

and archaeology work as crew chiefs. We worked together to create field and museum protocols to meet management and research goals. While April focused on children and childrearing in camp and Dana on changing conceptions of femininity, my focus was the camp's landscape and its gardens in particular (Clark, Kamp-Whittaker, and Shew 2008). Because much of their day was devoted to overseeing crews, the graduate students' research often took place in the late afternoon or evening. After an evening field excursion, April excitedly handed me an artifact she and Dana had found during their survey: a jar filled with seeds (figure 1.1).

The seeds contained in that jar are squash or perhaps gourd seeds. Both are among the kinds of plants former incarcerees recall being grown in camp gardens, and historic photographs capture some of the varieties produced in camp (figure 1.2). Among the donated items being documented at the museum that summer were gourds decorated with a variety of seeds (figure 1.3). Both the gourds and the seeds on them were grown at Amache. Some varieties of squash like *kabocha* are commonly grown in Japan, but the seeds in this jar could also represent species more easily acquired in the United States, such as pumpkins.

FIGURE 1.2. Historical photograph of squash and melons at the Amache Agricultural Fair, fall 1943. *Courtesy,* Amache Preservation Society, McClelland Collection, Granada, CO.

FIGURE 1.3. Decorated gourd from Amache, now in the collections of the Amache Museum. *Courtesy,* DU Amache Project.

FIGURE 1.4. Drawing of the maker's mark found on the base of the jar of saved seeds. *Courtesy*, DU Amache Project.

We found the jar itself quite tantalizing. Now a part of the permanent Amache collection, the base bears a maker's mark embossed there during manufacturing. The distinctive shape is associated with one of the primary bottle manufacturers of the twentieth century, the Owens-Illinois Glass Company. Surrounding the company symbol are numbers that represent the year the bottle was made and the location of the plant (figure 1.4). A quick look at a reference book (Toulouse 2001) told us that the jar was manufactured in 1937 in a plant in Los Angeles. Most jars of this sort contain food items that would not have lasted on the shelves even half of the five years that transpired between their manufacture and the outbreak of World War II. It seemed likely, then, that this jar was brought to camp by one of the thousands of incarcerees sent here from the Los Angeles area. If that was the case, then perhaps it came the way we found it: full of seeds. Regardless, it told us that at least one incarceree was in the habit of saving seeds and did so at Amache. A headline in the Japanese-language section of the Amache newspaper stating "Oriental Vegetable Seed Needed" (*Granada Pioneer* 1943a) suggests that individual was not alone.

Why Archaeology? Why Gardens?

Conducting archaeology at a site within living memory would seem counterintuitive. Not only are there survivors who remember the experience of their confinement, there are reams of government documents to be found in archives, in libraries, and online. There are also period records created by incarcerees, from letters to photographs to art. Even with this rich documentary and oral record, archaeology reveals a different story, finely textured with the material evidence of daily lives and the landscapes in which they were lived. The jar of seeds is a good example of how historical archaeology can contribute new insights into even well-known historical periods. It is among the many finds at Amache that reveal strategies and networks of action, drawing us into a story that would otherwise go untold.

That would be unfortunate because we need the lessons of the gardens and gardeners of Amache. As the displacement of peoples explodes across the globe, we can turn to Amache and its sister sites to understand how people under stress made effective places. There are lessons here for those who plan refugee and temporary worker camps or who want our prisons to be more humane.

The remains at Amache also speak to a broad public interested in history and civic justice. This place came about because of the dangerous combination of racism and fear, yet it contains eloquent expressions of dignity. When the temptation rises to single out groups as somehow less intrinsic to a body politic, Amache and the other Japanese American confinement sites remind us of the generational consequences of that act. In that vein, they are especially powerful touchstones for those who have a family history of confinement during World War II. As will be revealed in the pages to come, this work is deeply indebted to the community of former incarcerees and their families. This is not an easy heritage, and I hope my collaborators will see how much richer this work is because of their willingness to share their own and their families' stories.

Of all the topics that could be pursued at Amache, why gardens? Several answers intertwine like the morning glories once found at camp. Growing things was the primary occupation of Japanese Americans in 1940, whether they were farmers or gardeners or worked in a nursery. A focus on gardening helps us understand how they were taking that expertise and applying it to an entirely new landscape: the High Plains of Colorado. In addition, the remnants of gardens are one of the reasons the site has been recognized as a National Historic Landmark, a status reserved for the country's most significant historic locales. A focus on gardens also connects Amache to the broader experience of the World War II home front. This is particularly clear for the vegetable gardens that, both inside and outside the camp, were framed as "victory gardens." Finally, they are a way to see agency, initiative, and hope in a very dark time. Amache's gardens encourage all of us to invest in the future, to plant even if we are not ensured of a harvest.

This research came about in part because I live and work in Colorado, but Amache would be a good choice for any archaeologist. Of the ten primary Japanese American incarceration camps, it is among the best preserved, especially with regard to its landscape. There is also an active stakeholder community who works collaboratively with scholars. Finally, there is strong community support for preservation of this site and the items associated with it. They are thoughtfully managed by the people of nearby Granada, Colorado. Readers who are inspired by this work can take the opportunity to visit the site and museum.

Finding Solace in the Soil: A Preview

The title of this book, *Finding Solace in the Soil*, has a dual meaning. On one hand, it reflects a key assertion about gardens at Amache or any of the other locations where people of Japanese ancestry were incarcerated during World War II. Gardens were a pathway to solace in a time of upheaval. The title is also inspired by archaeological practice, the search for physical evidence of past human action. Like gardening, archaeology often requires digging, but our harvest is knowledge. This book tacks back and forth, focusing at times on the search for the gardens and at others on what has been found.

Much like the sediment that surrounds a buried garden, a scholar's work also exists in a matrix. This includes theories and methods that have been tested over time. When concerned with human behavior, the culture of those studied—traditions, history, belief systems—must always be accounted for. As an archaeologist, that matrix is physical, too; the discipline requires concern with the location of our finds and the physical conditions that affect their preservation. As a social scientist, the larger public context of this study is also never far from my mind. How do people interact with this history? What work does this site of heritage do today?

A concern with the lived experience of diverse populations has long been an anchor of the field of historical archaeology. The work of a generation of scholars provides a foundation for what is presented here (e.g., Deetz 1996; Singleton 1999; Wall 1991). Methodologically, it owes much to the archaeology of gardens and landscapes (e.g., Currie 2005; Malek 2013; Yamin and Metheny 1996). But because it engages with survivors, it also pushes this work into territory more typically connected with cultural anthropology (e.g., Castañeda and Mattews 2008; Slaughter 2006). Indeed, it is part of a growing movement of work which posits that the contemporary should be as much of a concern for archaeologists as the past (e.g., Harrison and Schofield 2010; Shanks and McGuire 1996). Chapter 2 further explores disciplinary inspiration and lays out the specific methods employed in this work.

The cultural and historical context of this research follows. In chapter 3, readers are introduced to the Japanese homeland, with a focus on gardening and farming in Japan. This context serves as a foundation to better understand those who left Japan for the United States. Through exploring communities and work patterns, it evidences both global connections and local strategies.

The forced removal and incarceration of Japanese Americans during World War II is the focus of chapter 4. It begins with an overview of the disturbing chain of events following Pearl Harbor. Then it shifts to focus specifically on Amache, one of the ten War Relocation Authority camps. It provides critical detail about the physical and social structure of the camp to frame the research done there.

After setting the stage, the book shifts into the heart of its tale: the gardens and gardeners of Amache. Chapter 5 focuses on two populations whose contributions to the transformation of the camp's landscape are still very evident: nursery professionals and children. It is an exploration of intergenerational ways the raw military setting of Amache became something that looked a whole lot more like a town.

How the gardens at Amache evidence connections at multiple spatial scales is the focus of chapter 6. It begins with families and then considers connections within the barracks blocks. Especially through the materials employed, gardens also evidence community-wide connections. The scale then moves out to beyond the camp, investigating both the physical and social landscapes of wartime and how they shape what we find at Amache.

In chapter 7, I discuss the most widespread of the garden types at Amache: entryway gardens located adjacent to individual barracks. Research at the camp illuminates the wide variety in these gardens and in the gardeners who made them. Close attention to our results reveals insights into the roots of these gardens in Japanese tradition as well as often surprising innovations. During a time of material shortage and financial hardship, flexibility made tradition possible.

The final interpretive chapter draws all the research results together to answer a key question: Why did incarcerees invest so much in gardens? In chapter 8, I posit that gardens and gardening met key needs for those imprisoned at Amache and other confinement camps. Improvements in the local environment came about by creating microclimates, reducing blowing sand, and providing better food to eat. As a dispossessed people, incarcerees needed to feel some stability, and gardening was a way to literally put down roots. Gardening was also an embodied act and thus an ideal way for physically active people to pass the time. Finally, gardening met spiritual needs of incarcerees, such as the need for beauty, for a connection to nature, and for balance.

The epilogue brings our story back to the present with the suggestion that the gardens of Amache can be thought of as *giri*, a Japanese concept with overtones of gift and obligation. They are a gift in that they provide a storehouse of knowledge about how to create beauty without waste, how to translate design principles in a new setting, and how to grow plants in an inhospitable environment. They are also an avenue to understand how people can maintain their dignity in a situation that dehumanizes them. Yet the gardens are also an obligation. We need to study and interpret them with care, and we need to preserve them as a testimony for the future.

After the epilogue are two resources the reader may find useful. The first is a taxa table, a list of the plants this research has identified as likely to have been grown at Amache. The second is a glossary of terms that may be unfamiliar to readers. It covers technical archaeology terms, words in Japanese, and terms relating to the history of Amache.

A Note on Terminology

The words used to describe the experience of the wartime removal and incarceration of Japanese Americans are exceptionally fraught (Daniels 2008). During the war, the US government employed many forms of propaganda to portray its actions in the best light possible. The terminology employed was the kind of double-speak that would have made George Orwell cringe. US citizens of Japanese ancestry were referred to as "non-aliens," people who were not faced with a natural disaster were nonetheless "evacuated" from their homes. The temporary prisons in which they were first placed were "assembly centers," while their final confinement camps were called "relocation centers." The experience has been glossed as "internment" and indeed the National Park Service, which manages and maintains three of the War Relocation Authority (WRA) camps, often employs this mid-ground term. When trying to connect with the general public, its use makes sense because it is the term with which most people are familiar.

Yet technically speaking, internment involves the lawful detaining of enemy aliens. It is a process governed by both national statutes and international law. This term correctly applies to the 8,000 or so Japanese nationals who were detained by the US Department of Justice (Daniels 2008). Not only was there a federal policy in place to detain such individuals, but detainees were given the chance for hearings in which they could be cleared and released. The remainder of those rounded up by the United States cannot technically be "internees" because they were either US citizens or were not given the chance for trial. Their experience parallels a different model—concentration camps—where ethnic or other minorities are confined without judicial recourse. This was, in fact, a term used for the Japanese American camps in some of the more frank correspondence of US officials, including President Franklin D. Roosevelt (Daniels 1972). Many Japanese American organizations, for example, the Japanese American Citizens League (2013), have endorsed a policy to refer to the WRA facilities as "American concentration camps." Yet not everyone agrees with that policy, in no small part because when US officials used that term earlier in World War II, it had not yet become conflated with the Nazi death camps (Daniels 2008).

My conversations with survivors and their descendants suggest a similar ambivalence. One issue with calling these facilities "concentration camps" is that the choice can alienate important stakeholders both at the larger public level and within specific important groups, in particular local residents who live with these sites and the families of those who worked at the camps. In a book like this, where the goal is to open up history to as wide an audience as possible, avoiding a term that often shuts down dialogue seems prudent. So here I take a compromise position, understanding that compromise rarely makes anyone happy. Throughout this manuscript I use the terms *incarceration* or *confinement* unless citing period documents. Likewise, those who were unlawfully confined are typically referred to as incarcerees or detainees. If some are offended by my choices, I hope they understand that they were made in good faith and with full knowledge that the stakes around this history remain painfully high (Clark 2016).

2

Studying Amache's Gardens
Methodology and Practice

In preparation for the first field school to be held at Amache in 2008, I traveled to the site with Dr. Robert "Buck" Sanford, a colleague from the Department of Biology at the University of Denver. An ecologist interested in how nutrients move through the ecosystem, Buck generously came to Amache to help me better understand the soils there. We drove the site talking about the people who had lived there and stopped to examine several of the possible garden locations I wanted to explore that year. Buck turned to me at some point and said something I have never forgotten: "This soil is an artifact." We went on to set up a series of soil chemistry tests, brainstorming ways to capture the soils management strategies of those imprisoned at Amache, as well as the ecological processes of a region just coming out of the Dust Bowl.

I will be forever grateful to Buck because what he said to me that day flipped a cognitive switch. Like most archaeologists, I have been trained in how to analyze more traditional "artifacts," the most common definition being individual objects crafted by people. But another definition, the one I teach my students, is that artifacts include not just things *made* by humans,

DOI: 10.5876/9781646420933.c002

like ceramics, but also things *modified* by humans, like a piece of sharpened bone. So although Buck may have been stretching the definition to make his point, he was, in fact, correct. What he implied, and something I have taken to heart in directing the work at Amache, is that just like the homemade coal scoops found on the surface of the site, the soils at Amache are the product of incarceree ingenuity and must be respected and carefully studied. They are a critical part of Amache's legacy for us today.

Yet even before Buck joined me at the site, my thoughts about the landscape at Amache were being shaped by other scholars. At the beginning stages of the project, my friend and colleague Steven Archer was leading archaeological investigations of the gardens at the College of William and Mary in Williamsburg, Virginia (Archer et al. 2015). As I discussed with him my interest in Amache and especially the gardens there, Steve insisted that I needed to employ the rigorous methodologies developed over the years by practitioners of garden archaeology. That was a specialization with which I had some familiarity; my dissertation research had involved a landscape-based approach to a Hispanic settlement in southern Colorado (Clark 2011). But certainly, unlike Steve, I was no expert in the archaeological study of gardens, so I began to study up on that literature (e.g., Currie 2005; Malek 2013). Steve and I then worked together to come up with a research design and methodological approach suited to such a complex landscape. Key to success has been Steve's presence onsite each season to help design the excavations and to train crews in the craft of garden excavation.

This chapter overviews the garden archaeology at Amache as it has evolved over six field seasons. It frames what my crews and I have found and how we came to understand it. It is part of the effort of public scholarship to not just illuminate findings but also to clarify how conclusions are reached.

The Written, the Remembered, and the Wrought

There are three different types of information about the gardens at Amache. The first, the written, is the stuff of historians. We find it in books and archives. The remembered is what we can learn from talking to people, about both their own and their family's stories. Finally, there is what archaeologists specialize in: objects and place made by people, the wrought. At Amache the searches for these three types of data are intricately intertwined;

as one source answers and then raises questions, one can turn to another and another.

What I turned to first was the historical record. These sources inform much of what you will read in the next two chapters. When I started, only one published work, *Amache: The Story of Japanese Internment in Colorado during World War II* by Robert Harvey (2003), focused entirely on the history of the camp.[1] Several chapters of Kiyo Hirano's memoir *Enemy Alien* (1983) cover her time at Amache. More recently, artist Lily Havey (2014) has produced a "creative memoir" about her Amache experience. The wartime letters and diaries of Yamato Ichihashi, a professor at Stanford who spent a portion of the war at Amache, provide a period look at camp life (Chang 1997). Other books that discuss Amache in some detail include two community histories of the Yamato colonies (Matsumoto 1993; Noda 1981) as well as Bill Hosokawa's book about Japanese Americans in Colorado (2005). For information about the physical structure of the camp, I turned to forms written in support of Amache's designation as a National Historic Landmark (Simmons and Simmons 1993, 2004). Perhaps the most important source for me, because it is what drew my attention to the site's rich archaeological potential, was a report written by the team that performed a preliminary survey of the site in 2003 (Carrillo and Killam 2004). That report documented specific gardens or likely garden features, but nearly all of these sources discussed the gardens at Amache.

Archival sources include official War Relocation Authority (WRA) reports about the confinement camps and specifically Amache. Many community materials, such as the camp newspapers, were gathered years ago by the University of California, Berkeley. Invaluable to our investigations are the many photographs taken in the camps. Official WRA photographs are often available online, while the other works of photographers are held by individual archives. Despite the early restrictions on cameras in camp, many incarcerees documented their experience photographically (Peterson 2018). Many of these photos have been digitized and are available through online repositories such as Densho (www.densho.org) and the University of California's Calisphere (www.calisphere.org). But as I started this

---

1   A number of my former incarceree collaborators also contributed to the Harvey book. Although an important source, they note that the book contains a number of errors and inconsistencies, especially regarding people's names.

work, the most important source for such images was community members themselves.

My entrée into the world of Amache was John Hopper, whose work preserving Amache and all that is associated with it has been widely recognized, from preservation awards to a medal from the Emperor of Japan. A social studies teacher in the Granada schools, John saw engagement with Amache as an important way for his students to connect to local history (Otto 2009). At his urging, students began to interview local residents who had either been incarcerated at the camp or worked there. John also contacted many former Amache incarcerees to elicit information and memorabilia. Those contacts and others began donating both documents and objects associated with Amache to John. Under the auspices of the local school district, John and district officials formed the Amache Preservation Society (APS), which is both part of the school curriculum and a nonprofit organization.[2] Not only did John give me (and later my students) full access to his collections, he also gave me a list of people to contact as I embarked on this work.

At the top of his list was Minoru "Min" Tonai, whose recollections are woven into many chapters in this book. Min is the president of the Amache Historical Society, the largest organization of former Amache incarcerees. With support from my university, I was able to travel to Los Angeles to meet with him and other members of the historical society. Over several days I engaged many people in conversations about life in camp, about the gardens there, and about how archaeology there should proceed. Those were invaluable meetings that continue to shape my thinking about and research on Amache.

During that first trip to Los Angeles, several former Amacheans, especially Thomas Shigekuni, insisted that I meet Jack Muro. As a young man, Jack was among those who arrived early to Amache to help build the camp. Despite its being contraband, he successfully acquired a camera, which he used to extensively document the camp over the years. Not only did he take pictures at Amache, he also developed and in some cases printed them there in a darkroom he excavated under his barrack (Ono 2013). Among his many jobs in camp, Jack used to climb up the camp water tower to check the water level.

---

2   Readers interested in the work of the Amache Preservation Society are encouraged to visit its website at www.amache.org.

FIGURE 2.1. A portion of Jack Muro's Amache photograph scrapbook. These are all hand-cut images from 35 mm proof sheets. *Courtesy,* Jack Muro.

That vantage point provided a view that inspired many photographs. Taken over the course of the camp's history, they capture the evolving camp land-scape. Like many of the early arrivals, Jack lived in Block 6H, the location of the Amache Town Hall. As will be discussed in greater detail in chapter 6, an extensive public garden was built adjacent to the town hall. Jack's pho-tographs beautifully capture that garden (and the people who enjoyed it) at different times of the year. I am exceptionally grateful to Jack for sharing with me many of his photographs, some of which only existed as negatives and proof prints (figure 2.1). Gary Ono, another former Amache incarceree, is making sure that others can benefit from this extensive photo archive. A retired professional photographer and now volunteer with the Japanese American National Museum in Los Angeles, Gary has been working tire-lessly with Jack to scan and document his collection.

A number of other individuals, some of them associated with the Amache Historical Society, shared photographs that they or their families had held onto since camp. Among the most important for this work were pictures of gardens. These photos, which can often be tied to specific locations at Amache, have proven invaluable. In the cases where the owners recall gardens or gar-dening in camp, those photographs led to oral histories with the donors. These conversations helped me more effectively weave people into this account.

Another important source of visual documentation of the Amache land-scape arrived at the APS museum a few years ago. During the war, Masaki "Sam" Nakashima took a series of 16 mm movies at Amache, both in color

FIGURE 2.2. Cook in an Amache mess hall garden ringing a gong to announce a meal. This still was captured from a 16 mm movie made at Amache. *Courtesy,* Amache Preservation Society, Tsukuda Collection, Granada, CO.

and in black and white. Mr. Nakashima was from Woodland, California, and lived in Block 8E, Barrack 10F with his wife, Natsuye. The films reveal daily life in camp, like people lining up for meals in the mess hall or children playing near barracks. Some capture historic moments, like the aftermath of a mess hall fire. Unfortunately, it is difficult to recover crisp stills from the footage, but even the blurry images reveal a wide variety of Amache's gardens and people's interactions with them (figure 2.2). Where appropriate, those images are interspersed in this book.

Scholarship about the experience of internment put the Amache data into context. I was inspired in my own research by that of landscape architect Anna Tamura, who as a graduate student studied gardens at Manzanar and Minidoka. She forcefully argues that camp gardens are "precious cultural resources" that express "raw creativity and ingenuity in action" (Tamura 2004, 19). Other inspiration came from Jeffrey F. Burton, coauthor of *Confinement and Ethnicity,* which showcases the archaeological potential of all ten WRA camps (Burton et al. 2002). Dr. Burton kindly advised me from the outset of the project, and the archaeology of gardens and landscaping at

Manzanar with which he has been involved (Burton 2015) provides important comparisons for research at Amache. Kenneth I. Helphand's book *Defiant Gardens* (2006) places the WRA camp gardens into the context of institutional confinement—for example, by comparing them to the gardens at prison camps. As reflected in chapter 3 of this book, there is also significant scholarship on Japanese gardens globally. In particular, Kendall H. Brown's work (1999, 2013) on Japanese-style gardens in the United States shaped my approach at Amache. A site visit by Dr. Brown in 2014 sharpened my understanding of the unique resources at Amache and connected me to the North American Japanese Gardens Association, an organization dedicated to studying and nurturing Japanese-style gardens. Participation in the association's 2016 conference on the healing power of these gardens reaffirmed my nascent interpretations of Amache's archaeology.

Research Design and Methodology

Both as an ethical obligation and as a logistical one, the creation of a research design should precede any archaeological investigation. This is true of the DU Amache Project, which is unique within research on the ten WRA sites through its long-term collaborative approach and the integration of a field school. As discussed in the introduction to this chapter, the project started with a commitment to landscape-based inquiry but has also been shaped by the research interests of graduate students gathering data for their theses.[3]

The initial research design for the first field school in 2008 was based on existing documentation, conversations with stakeholders, and in-person reconnaissance. Historic photographs of the site and the 2003 archaeology survey indicated that a number of partially buried garden features still existed at Amache. To organize their study, I classified the gardens into the three categories that seemed to be most common at Amache and that are also often found at other camps (Helphand 2006; Tamura 2004): public space ornamental gardens, vegetable gardens, and entryway gardens found

3 As of this writing, eleven theses by University of Denver master's students have been completed on Amache. The research design, methodology, and results presented here focus on Amache's landscape, but interested readers can access those MA theses, as well as our full research designs and field season reports, through the University of Denver's digital Amache collection: https://digitalcommons.du.edu/amache/.

adjacent to individual barracks. To better understand these different types of gardens as they were created at Amache, I planned test excavations in at least one of each type of feature for that first year in the field. That plan would also help test a set of methods for the discovery and study of these gardens.

Archaeology crews began that year, as they have in each subsequent field season, with a systematic pedestrian survey, a common archaeological technique wherein investigators walk across the landscape at a set distance from one another, looking for artifacts and other physical evidence of past human behavior. At Amache, survey crews walk at a 2 meter interval—almost fingertip to fingertip—a very intensive level of investigation. While walking, crew members call out each non-structural artifact they come across and note evidence of modifications to the camp landscape. An inventory of artifacts and landscape features is created during this process, and findings that need to be mapped (which include all features and artifacts with further data potential) are flagged. Subsequent digital mapping creates detailed spatial documentation of the phenomena discovered by that year's crews. Those results are uploaded into a geographic information system (GIS) database. That database makes it possible to compile multiple years of research, something important for a long-term project like the Amache work. Using GIS, our results can be overlain on base maps such as aerial photographs, which reveal extant trees, building foundations, and roadways. Crews also map a selection of features by hand to capture their small-scale detail (figure 2.3). Surveys are organized by the historical division of the camp, which is individual blocks. That first year, as with subsequent years, our choice of blocks to survey was driven both by my interest in gardens and by the research of my graduate students (Clark, Kamp-Whittaker, and Shew 2008). Our work has primarily focused on blocks where incarcerees lived but also in public-area blocks.

Once potential features we might want to investigate further have been identified either through survey, historical research, or both, our next step is to employ ground-penetrating radar (GPR). The integral role of GPR in this project has been made possible by my colleague Dr. Lawrence (Larry) Conyers. Larry is a pioneer in the application of GPR to archaeology and has included the studies at Amache in several of his publications (e.g., 2012). During each field season he has kindly volunteered his time and equipment so crews can experience how this low-impact technique can help us "see" below the surface of the ground. It has also been a key component of many

FIGURE 2.3. Students sketching a landscaping feature at Amache (Block 6H), summer 2008. For an example of a garden sketch map, see figure 5.4a. *Courtesy,* DU Amache Project.

of the MA theses completed at Amache (Driver 2015; Garrison 2015; Kamp-Whittaker 2010; Starke 2015).

GPR involves pulling a box-like antenna and receiver over the ground (figure 2.4). It sends electromagnetic waves into the soil and records the rate at which they return. If those waves encounter a change in moisture, such as happens with a compact surface, a buried wall, or concentrations of artifacts, the waves are reflected at different rates (Conyers 2013, 27). Before running the GPR unit, crews set up a measured grid oriented to the camp layout and tied into our overall site map. Being systematic about its use means GPR can be used to map the subsurface both in plan, which is a view from overhead, and in profile, like the view from the bank of a river. With the graphics created by GPR, the extent, location, and physical integrity of buried features like walls, fences, and compact surfaces can be assessed.

GPR is a time-intensive exercise, especially at Amache where the native vegetation is brushy and lifts the unit off the ground. After some flawed attempts, it became obvious that to get good data, crews needed to clear off

FIGURE 2.4. DU Amache crews doing ground-penetrating radar in an entryway garden (Block 11H), summer 2012. *Courtesy,* DU Amache Project.

much of the surface vegetation in any GPR survey area. Although this is one of the crew's least favorite activities, it also has the added benefit of making the surface much more visible, a boon when deciding where to place excavation units. After brush clearance, previously unseen garden walls, landscaping stone, and surface artifacts are often discovered.

If the GPR suggests further analysis could be fruitful, the next step is to lay out test excavation units tied into the GPR grid. Large areas are needed to reveal how gardens were planned, so excavation units in the Amache gardens are typically 2 meters on each side. We often lay out excavation units in a checkerboard-type pattern (figure 2.5) to reveal aspects of garden design, such as symmetry or the lack thereof. This allows us to cover more area of a garden than a block of units; if something interesting, like a walkway or a planting hole for a tree, extends into an adjacent unit, crews can expand the excavations, filling in the gaps.

FIGURE 2.5. Crews during test excavations of a garden bed in Block 9L, summer 2008. *Courtesy,* DU Amache Project.

Excavating a garden is time-intensive and requires focus. Crews carefully remove soil either with a flat-faced shovel or a trowel. Important artifacts or landscaping elements found in place are mapped and, where appropriate, collected. The soil removed is painstakingly screened with a small (⅛ inch mesh), which aids in the recovery of small artifacts and sometimes seeds. If interior garden features or compelling artifacts are elusive, it can be frustrating, but I remind the crew of Sanford's adage: the soil is an artifact. They are uncovering it, slowly and systematically.

Once excavations are below the roots of small surface plants like bunch grass, crews begin to systematically take soil samples. These samples serve several purposes. The larger soil samples (10 liters) are designed to recover what is known as macrobotanical remains: the pieces of plants that are visible to the eye, like stems and seeds. Smaller soil samples (about a handful's worth) are taken to assess the chemistry of the recovered soil in the laboratory. That analysis seeks information on the kinds of nutrients that assist in plant growth, like nitrogen, phosphorous, and organic carbon (Miller and Gleason 1994). Crews are trained to look for situations in which an item in the garden (like a stepping stone) could have blocked rain from the soil underneath, thus preserving the pollen in place. In those instances, crews carefully take about a half cup of soil, which will be sent to the project palynologist, Dr. John G. Jones, who specializes in the study of pollen recovered from archaeological sites.

Despite trial and error, the success of the 2008 garden investigations suggested it was a research program worth following. By 2010, these four research questions drove the work:

1. How were incarcerees applying their horticultural and agricultural expertise to this new environment? For example, were they amending the poor soil of the camp and, if so, how?
2. What types of strategies for transforming the military environment are evident both in the hardscaping and plant remains of the gardens?
3. How do the gardens fit into the larger picture of life in confinement?
4. Are there intact gardens or landscaping that might be impacted by planned improvements to the site, such as the return of historical structures?

Three gardens were chosen for analysis in 2010: one vegetable garden and two entryway gardens. The entryway gardens excavated in 2008 were at the elementary school, so in 2010 the research design focused on gardens located immediately in front of incarceree-occupied barracks. We chose one entryway garden photographed at the time the camp was occupied and another identified during site survey. The vegetable garden chosen for analysis was visible in historical photographs. It was also adjacent to the footers for the camp's water tower, which has since been renovated and returned to the camp. Better understanding of that garden's location and significance assisted site managers in protecting the area during construction activities in this vicinity. Crews from my university were also joined that summer by Dr. Erika Marín-Spiotta and Emily C. Eggleston of the University of Wisconsin–Madison. They refined our techniques for soil chemistry analysis while also gathering data for Emily's master's thesis (Eggleston 2012).

In each of the next subsequent field schools, 2012 and 2014, crews excavated an entryway garden per year, each of them incorporating a different type of design than those studied in prior years. In 2016 crews tested another public garden, this time a feature that ran along the back of a barrack but facing the historical road along the block's edge. The summer of 2018 found

TABLE 2.1. Excavated gardens discussed in this book

Block	Barrack or Feature #	Type	Associated Gardeners	Year Tested
7G	5F	Entryway	Mataji Umeda	2010
8H	Feature 1	School entryway	Elementary students	2008
8H	Feature 2	School entryway	Elementary students	2008
9L	Feature 1	Public ornamental		2008
11F	Recreation hall	Landscaping		2018
11H	9E/9F	Entryway	Zenkichi Sairyo Kahichi Yokoi	2012
11H	1	Public ornamental	Denzaburo Kishi	2016
12H	5F	Entryway	Saichiro and Bun Hirota	2010
12H	6F	Entryway	Chozaburo and Ai Okumura	2014
12K	Feature VG-1	Vegetable		2008
12K	Feature VG-2	Vegetable		2010

crews once again excavating ahead of site improvements. We worked in the area surrounding a historical recreation hall that had just been returned to its original location at Amache. Stabilization of the building required grading the current ground surface, but a 2016 survey had identified a tree alignment to the south of that building. By focusing our excavation in that area, we could better understand the extent and nature of the landscaping so it can be better protected during future work on the building.

Over the course of six field seasons, we had tested at least two of each type of garden found at Amache, with a focus on the small-scale entryway gardens (table 2.1). That focus came about because of pedestrian survey, which as of 2018 had covered 26 blocks in total: 21 barracks blocks, 3 developed public blocks (including the elementary school), and 2 undeveloped blocks used as informal trash dumps (figure 2.6). That systematic look indicates that entryway gardens are the most common type still to be found at Amache. To understand gardens and gardening in this unwilling community, they are key.

Once the fieldwork is over, research in the lab begins. Even before leaving the field, crews process some of the samples. To study botanical remains, like seeds or wood fragments, they need to be separated from the rest of the soil collected. This is made easier by the simple fact that organic materials float. So crews put the soil into a tank and agitate it, capturing what floats to the

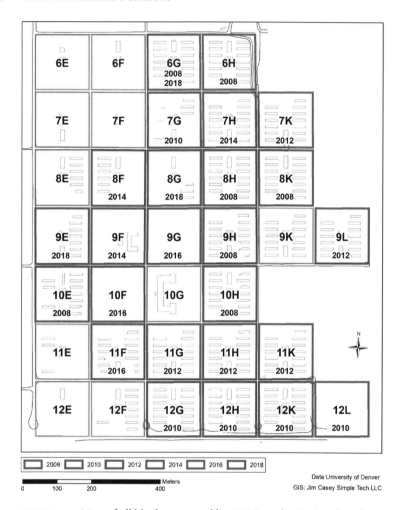

FIGURE 2.6. Map of all blocks surveyed by DU Amache Project (as of 2018). *Courtesy,* Jim Casey.

top in a mesh bag (this is known as light fraction). It is carefully dried and then sent to Steven Archer, the project archaeobotanist, for analysis. Most of the smaller grains of sand wash through the system, but the bottom of the flotation tank is lined with window screen. The items captured by the screen (the heavy fraction) are saved for later sorting.

Students in my courses at the University of Denver do the lion's share of the analysis of artifacts collected both from the surface and from excavations.

Their results are entered into a database that has now been built up with six field seasons of data. They also sort through the heavy fraction, looking to see if artifacts are present. While my students are working with the artifacts, project specialists are doing their work to analyze botanical, pollen, and soil chemistry data recovered from excavations.

Lab work with the tangible remains of the camp often sends my students and me back to our other sources of data—to photographs of the camp, to the newspaper published there, and to community members. Tacking back and forth between different data sets, trying to integrate them, is what makes historical archaeology challenging and fascinating but also an ongoing exercise (Wilkie 2006). There are always more sources to consult, more data to synthesize.

3

Japanese Gardens and Diaspora

I've visited Japanese-style gardens from Brooklyn to Boca Raton, but perhaps my favorite is also the least known. The southeast coastline of Hawaii (the Big Island) is currently home to black sand beaches and sea turtles. But the cultural landscape reveals the remains of numerous sugar plantations, where ethnically diverse populations worked physically taxing jobs together. The Honoapu plantation, like most such facilities throughout the island chain, included a significant proportion of Japanese workers. In their rare spare time, some of these workers transformed a chiefly Hawaiian fish pond into a strolling garden complete with a bridge and a stone lantern. Although the plantation is gone and the garden is no longer maintained, it is still a lovely location for contemplation, with its undulating shoreline and sojourns by the sea turtles. During my visit a fish leaped out of the pond and into the air, reminding me of one way gardens and Buddhist beliefs are connected. For believers, leaping fish are models of the perseverance needed to attain enlightenment (Slawson 1987, 124).

The Honoapu garden highlights the fact that people of Japanese descent have created gardens all over the world, often in trying circumstances. These

DOI: 10.5876/9781646420933.c003

gardens are adapted to local settings but share a deep genealogy through both the ideas and the people behind them. To truly appreciate these places, one needs cultural context for both the Japanese-style garden and the Japanese diaspora. A term employed by scholars from many disciplines (e.g., Butler 2001), diaspora refers to the phenomenon of multiple generations spread far from a homeland but with effective and affective ties to the place and people of their ancestry. With a real pride in heritage and tradition, Nikkei, or overseas Japanese, provide a good example of a diasporic community (Adachi 2006). The spread of Japanese-style gardens is one marker of their extent and impact.

The Japanese Landscape

This tale begins in Japan, a series of mostly temperate and mountainous islands in the west Pacific. The climate and topography ensure that dense forest is the natural vegetation cover, although through millennia of agricultural and urban development, people have carved out agricultural terraces, cities, and harbors. Traditional occupations of farming, forestry, and fishing were reliant on the natural resources of this volcanic archipelago. Nature, for many Japanese, is a "benevolent force to be trusted" (Havens 1974, 14). Many scholars (e.g., Holborn 1978) identify a veneration of the natural as the basis on which Japanese garden philosophy is founded. This finds expression in many ways—for example, in the elegant lines of *suiseki*, unmodified stones set in stands for contemplation. It happens cyclically, as city dwellers fill the parks to see the first of the cherry blossoms or to collect leaves in the fall. In small villages, this respect is expressed in annual rites related to the agricultural cycle.

The veneration of nature finds perhaps its fullest expression in Shintoism, which is both an organized religion and a philosophical outlook. Beginning as an animistic set of folk beliefs and practices, Shinto's first written appearance is in Imperial court documents that predate the sixth-century arrival of Buddhism in Japan (Reader 1993). In Shinto (or the "Way of the Gods"), natural elements are endowed with holiness or spirit known as *kami*. *Kami* dwells in such grand places as hilltops or mountains but also in smaller things like individual stones and trees. Shinto shrines can take a variety of forms: cleared locations in a forest setting spread with gravel and planted with sacred trees or even individual, natural stones, made visible as *iwakura*, or sacred rocks, through their decoration.

These Shinto shrines appear to be the prototypes of the Japanese garden. Indeed, the first written appearance of the word *niwa* (now a term for garden) described a sacred locale, purified for worship. This account of *niwa* comes from an early history (the *Nihon Shoki*), which notes that these early gardens were located within the palace complexes of Japan's Imperial families, dating back to the early centuries A D (Hayakawa 1973). Masao Hayakawa (1973, 27, 29) notes that it is very likely that trees or stones were central to the early *niwa* in the same fashion they were in Shinto shrines: "This sense of the holiness of natural beauty has figured importantly in the development of the Japanese garden." In this era farmers, who spent their entire lives interlocked with natural processes, saw nature as a benevolent, protective force. Farming hamlets were guarded by a local Shinto deity known as an *ujigami* (Fukutake 1980). The *ujigami* were beseeched at key moments, such as the first planting of rice, and were recognized for their generosity at harvest.

The history of Japan is marked by its people's openness to concepts and practices from the greater Asian sphere. The *Nihon Shoki* also notes that Buddhism was introduced through gifts from Korea, including a statue and texts (Reader 1993). The kanji script, as well as Confucian philosophy, came by way of China. Ideas about gardens also filtered in from China, building on the foundation of Shinto philosophy especially as expressed in shrines. By the establishment in late A D 700 of the new Imperial capital of Heiankyo (now known as Kyoto), aristocratic residences typically included large gardens replete with ponds for boating and islands on which musicians could entertain guests. Strongly influenced by the powerful T'ang dynasty, these gardens served a similar purpose to those in China—providing beauty to residents but also functioning as arenas in which visitors could be both entertained and impressed (Slawson 1987).

The earliest of the written Japanese gardening guides, the *Sakuteiki*, was compiled during the Heian period (A D 794–1185). Probably written by a series of authors from A D 1000 to 1100, it outlines the compiled knowledge of 200 years of garden making in Kyoto (Takei and Keane 2001). The city was designed on a grid plan, and properties were generally square. Gardens were a way to naturalize that environment, softening the hard symmetry of geometric town planning. Not only did gardens bring nature to the city, but, more important, they brought harmony with life forces. As Jirō Takei and Marc P. Keane (2001, 102) note in their translation of the work, "Garden design was, to some degree, perceived as a means of creating a balanced, protective environment within which the household existed."

To seek that balance, designers were encouraged to use nature as their model and to take advantage of existing features in the garden site. In contrast with gardening traditions in Europe, the guide notes that the making of a garden begins with the setting of stones. Although cast within Buddhist philosophy, the Shinto overtones are hard to miss. While acknowledging the power of stone, the *Sakuteiki* also notes that trees, especially old ones, have great value. Indeed, a site with many old, fine trees is better suited to be a temple or a shrine than a residence. Large Kyoto households might even have their own *komori*, or tree guardians (Takei and Keane 2001).

In his study of the rituals of the Heian period, Michel Vieillard-Baron (2007) asserts that by the tenth century, the Japanese had developed a cycle of rites, many associated with gardens. In aristocratic homes—as exemplified by the Imperial household—a combination of personal, familial, and ceremonial rituals took place, often in the courtyard space between the house and the central garden pond. Many of these rituals were calendrical (for example, marking the second day of the second month of the year), but others were exceptional, like prayers for rain during times of drought. As Vieillard-Baron (2007, 61) notes, these rituals tended to employ Shinto, Buddhist, and Ying-Yang practices simultaneously. Gardens were particularly well-suited as a locale for ritual intercession, he notes, because they exist as an intermediary space between the human-made world and the world of nature. The Heian was a time of political unrest in Japan, and Hayakawa (1973, 36) tells us that gardens became "a place of consolation and hope for people subjected to uncertainty and danger in their daily lives."

As exemplified by the *Sakuteiki*, Buddhist imagery and concepts were well woven into garden design and philosophy in the Heian period. During this time, gardens were often designed to evoke Buddhist paradise and other features of the Buddhist universe. For example, islands in ponds represented Mount Sumuru, the central mountain of the Buddhist cosmos (Ikagawa 1994, 32). Zen Buddhism, which arose during the subsequent Kamakura period (AD 1185–1333), brought a significant shift to garden design. Whereas earlier Buddhist-inspired gardens held realistic expressions of nature or representations of paradise, Zen Buddhist gardens presented nature in abstraction. Designing and maintaining gardens were also, like painting and meditation, forms of Zen religious practice (Berthier 2005).

Still cited by modern gardeners, Muso Soseki was the most important figure of medieval Japanese gardening (Hayakawa 1973, 59). A Buddhist priest, Soseki not only designed important gardens for Zen Buddhist temples, he also wrote and taught extensively. In Soseki's gardens, stones retain the importance placed on them in the *Sakuteiki* but for different reasons. They are not in themselves powerful; rather, they symbolize the transcendence desired by Zen practitioners. It was Soseki who designed the first known dry gardens, or *karesansui*, gardens that were not meant for moving through or acting in but for contemplation. In the subsequent Muromachi period (AD 1333–1573), these gardens became the standard for Buddhist temples, such as that at the Daisen-in, founded by the priest Kogaku in 1513 (Holborn 1978, 71). Kogaku wrote of the now famous *karesansui* garden there, "Only a man who has learned that God, or Buddha, helps those who help themselves is able to learn the lesson of the sand and of the rocks in the sand" (cited in Sobisha 1990, 20).

The next big innovation in Japanese garden design brought the garden back to the domestic realm and to a wide variety of people. Traditional Japanese homes are composed of a series of structures surrounded by a fenced enclosure. As one Western scholar noted during the 1800s, houses that often appeared quite plain on their street view opened onto meticulously designed gardens. It was facing the garden where the home's beautifully carved architectural elements might be found (Morse 1961 [1886]). These types of small gardens, which included a passageway from one building to another, found their fullest expression in the tea garden. First created during the Momoyama, or early modern period (AD 1573–1603), such gardens were part of a set of complex rituals known as "The Way of Tea." Not only did these rituals involve a prescribed suite of tea-preparation steps and artifacts, they gave rise to a specific architectural space—the *chaseki*, or teahouse. These were purposely plain structures that expressed two important aesthetics taught in the tea schools: *wabi*, an appreciation for that which is simple, even rustic; and *sabi*, admiration for items with the patina of age (Kurano 2016).

These aesthetics also shaped the passageway to the teahouse. In these spaces, gardens were meant to evoke a *roji*, or the dewy path one might find in a forest setting. Such gardens returned to earlier forms of Japanese gardens intended to evoke natural scenes. As one Momoyama period garden design guide notes, "In the planting of trees and herbs, you make their natural habitats your model" (Zōen n.d., entry 10). The reflection of nature was performed in very specific ways. The *roji* was not only an aesthetic space but a purposeful one. During the passage from the outside world to the teahouse, one needed to prepare for entering the world of tea by shedding the concerns of regular life. As one writer notes, "One of the most important aspects of the *roji* is the careful and deliberate attention with which it is designed to produce psychological changes in the people who walk through it" (Itoh 1973, 69). Designs were intended to focus the senses through elements like stepping stones that meandered rather than taking a direct path. Stone lanterns, sometimes collected from abandoned temples or shrines, were common in such gardens. Not only were they both *wabi* and *sabi*, they drew attention from passers-by, especially when lit at night. To evoke the sense of traveling through a forest, such gardens were not visible all at once; designers created illusions of depth through diverse plantings (Ikagawa 1994, 34). Tea gardens would become the most popular form of Japanese gardens (Eliovson 1970, 59), and their design ethos were adopted in domestic settings to such a great extent that one historian calls the tea garden "the model for the urban courtyard garden" (Itoh 1973, 70).

In the Edo period (AD 1603–1867), these different strains of garden design would come together in large strolling gardens or parks. The best of these gardens employed *shakkei*, or borrowed scenery. Although an element of design since antiquity, its use during this time was both more focused and deliberate, such as in the Enstu-ji garden in which trees were planted to frame mountain views (Hayakawa 1973, 140). Strolling gardens are those with which non-Japanese are most familiar, in no small part because they are the gardens most replicated abroad, especially in the era of the World's Fairs (Brown 1999). As crystalized after Japan opened to the West during the Meiji era (AD 1868–1912), many such gardens include pathways around large water features such as ponds and artificial waterfalls, raised hill forms, ornate bridges, stone lanterns, and aesthetically pruned trees.

It is interesting that strolling gardens were sometimes built in former rice paddies (Fujii 2014). Such siting took advantage of existing irrigation, essentially exchanging one form of artificial water feature for another. This is one of the few connections the garden literature makes to the landscapes with which Japanese of the pre-modern era were most familiar: rural villages and farms. Many of the same underlying philosophies—a closeness to nature, the belief in *kami*, the presence of shrines—link gardening and villages. Visits by rural Japanese to some of the larger shrines or temples with famous gardens were enabled by cooperative organizations (Fukutake 1980, 98). But still there appear to be only tantalizing hints that garden design philosophy had made its way to rural Japan by the Meiji era. This is reflected in particular in the writings of Edward Morse, hired in 1877 to teach zoology in Tokyo. With the avid eye of a scientist, he documented his four years in Japan in a series of books (Morse 1917, 1961 [1886]). He often noted that wherever he went, he encountered neat, carefully landscaped small gardens in the sort of side yards and backyards that in the Western world would be filled with rubbish or stray cats. He was particularly struck by the garden of one rather poorly furnished country inn: "In the room where our meal was served there was a circular window, through which could be seen a curious stone lantern and a pine-tree, the branches of which stretched across the opening, while beyond a fine view of some high mountains was to be had . . . wondering how so poor a house could sustain so fine a garden, I went to the window to investigate. What was my surprise to find that the extent of ground from which the lantern and pine-tree sprung was just three feet in width" (Morse 1961 [1886], 284). Rather less evocative was a more recent researcher of a specific Japanese village who spoke of houses with yards that are "simply packed earth except for the occasional flowers and shrubs" (Smith 1977, 35).

In an era when world cultures were ranked on the ladder of evolution, the Meiji government aimed to impress Western powers that it was a civilized nation. World's Fairs and other expositions provided a perfect opportunity to highlight Japanese culture and expand the world market for Japanese arts (Irvine 2013). Gardens were typically an integral part of these installations (Tagsold 2017). For example, the 1910 Japan-British Exhibition, held at the White City in London, featured two large gardens by Japanese designers. These gardens were visited by 8 million people, nearly 20 percent of Britain's entire population. The popularity and impact of such gardens can also be measured by the 100 or so Japanese-style gardens constructed in the United Kingdom in the first 50 years after the Meiji restoration (Raggett 2018).

Within Japan, the art of the Meiji era and the subsequent Taisho and Early Showa period (AD 1912–1945) was characterized by a fusion of Japanese tradition with Western design, materials, and techniques. The Japanese government sponsored global experts to teach and practice in Japan. A rallying cry was *wakon yosai*, or Japanese spirit, Western techniques (Irvine 2013, 167). Enthusiasm for Western art was widespread enough that concerns arose about the loss of Japanese cultural heritage. That call arose among some of the same Western scholars brought in to globalize Japan, such as Ernest Fenollosa, who was invited to teach philosophy and economics at Tokyo University but who became an important historian of Japanese art (Munsterberg 1978, 18). Garden design was similarly impacted during the Modern period; in particular, Western-style gardens could be found surrounding Western-style buildings. Many less overtly Western gardens were created for members of the new business class. Although not often interpreted as the apex of Japanese garden design, the infusion of new ideas during this time period did create "an undeniable freshness" (Hayakawa 1973, 143).

The Beginnings of Diaspora

Most histories of Japanese gardens end with the Meiji era the time when the first of the Japanese immigrants to America arrived. This is not a coincidence because both are linked to the same process: the opening of Japan to world trade and travel. After Commodore Perry forced a less than ideal trade agreement on the Japanese government in 1853, the government tottered for over a decade until 1867, when the final shogun surrendered authority to the royal family. Under the newly restored monarchy, Japan's formerly isolationist policy shifted radically. Japan was to be a modern, industrial state rather than the largely feudal society of its past. This represents a radical break in Japanese society. Indeed, pre-Meiji administrators aimed to keep farmers on the land rather than have them move into craft or trade (Havens 1974). Middle-class positions were seen as socially destabilizing, and peasants were encouraged to fulfill their destiny of raising crops.

But Japan faced a significant problem. Despite its temperate locale and volcanic geology, only 15 percent of the archipelago contains arable land, and even that is "deficient in natural fertility and irrigation" (Havens 1974, 11). Irrigation had been employed in the service of farming for millennia, but by the 1600s, 70 percent of agricultural irrigation currently in use was already in place (JCOLD 2009, 7). Without additional lands to move onto, rural families developed a system similar to that in other feudal agricultural settings. Only one child, typically but not always the oldest male heir, would inherit the farm (Smith 1977). Daughters would marry into other farming families and thus have a stable place in society. But younger sons of rural families had few choices. If their family was well-to-do, they might purchase additional lands and start a branch of the family tree, but for the most part these sons left their natal villages, presumably to work as laborers on other farms or in urban settings. As one study of rural villages asks, what happened to the departing sons (Smith 1977, 146)? During the Meiji period the answer was rather simple: they moved to cities to be part of Japan's industrial revolution or they emigrated.

The greatest number (approximately 270,000) of pre-World War II emigrants from Japan made their way to Manchuria, with Hawaii a close second at over 230,000 (Tsuchida 1998, 78). Until 1898, those who emigrated to Hawaii came to an independent nation. Labor recruiters from plantations, as well as Japanese-owned immigration companies, targeted rural areas of Japan for potential workers. These were often younger men but sometimes entire families. Recruiters for plantations promised free lodging and a food allowance, although, as many discovered, living conditions were often poor. Indeed, by 1894 the Japanese government stepped in with regulations to protect contract laborers by setting hours of work, provisions for a return passage, and requirements that employees not be treated cruelly (Hoobler and Hoobler 1996, 23).

Another important destination for Japanese emigrants was Brazil, with nearly 190,000 arriving by 1941 (Tsuchida 1998, 78). The United States was the only other country with over 100,000 Japanese emigrants. Although US law forbade immigrants from signing labor contracts before their arrival in the States, many immigration companies had arrangements with agents who recruited laborers as they disembarked. Industries that needed gangs of workers, such as railroads, mining, logging, and fish canneries, were among those who sought Japanese laborers (Hoobler and Hoobler 1996). Ironically, these were the same jobs that until the 1882 passage of the Chinese Exclusion Act were often filled by Chinese workers. After 1882, recruitment of Japanese laborers for these positions accelerated.

The Japanese government saw education abroad as one way to speed the development of the nation. They encouraged young men to emigrate for this purpose and screened them carefully, knowing they would represent their nation. This was also appealing to the men involved; they could expand their prospects while avoiding mandatory service in the military. Unless they were among the rare scholarship students supported by the Japanese government, these émigrés typically paid for their passage and education by working as domestic servants. Restricted by their economic need to work, many student laborers struggled to finish their education. But they were a significant vanguard, especially in urban areas. For example, in San Francisco, many important organizations, especially Japanese Christian churches and missions, were founded by these young immigrants (Ichioka 1988).

After completing their contracts or their education, many of these sojourners returned to Japan. However, many others found that they lacked the resources or the desire to do so. Urban centers like San Francisco and Seattle drew entrepreneurs looking to start businesses that catered to Japanese and other Asian customers. Other immigrants, especially those raised on farms in Japan, saw in agriculture opportunities for economic independence and mobility closed off in other sectors by anti-Asian unionism. This shift from labor to other pursuits happened primarily in the early years of the twentieth century; by 1909, more than 30,000 Japanese in California were involved in agriculture (Matsumoto 1993, 22). Farming in Japan was a labor-intensive rather than a land-intensive process, and those skills translated well to the West Coast of the United States. A focus on labor-intensive crops avoided by other farmers—berries, tomatoes, celery, and melons—translated to profits despite the often small parcels they worked.

Nikkei farmers and those in urban centers were linked through economic and social ties. For example, farmers and agricultural-related business owners forged powerful connections. The Seinan neighborhood of Los Angeles (discussed at more length later in this chapter) is a good example. It was home to produce markets and also truck farmers. In the San Francisco Bay area, Japanese growers came to virtually corner the flower market. Kyutaro Abiko, who would play an important role in the history of California, exemplified these connections. Abiko immigrated as a student in 1885 under the auspices of the Fukuinkai. A gospel society created by Methodist and Congregationalist converts, it provided members with lodging in San Francisco and, perhaps more important, the fellowship of other Japanese. Abiko became involved in several businesses, including the most widely circulated Japanese immigrant newspaper, *Nichibei Shimbun*. The paper was a platform for his ideals of a strong Japanese community to be built throughout California. This was not merely rhetoric for Abiko; in time, his firm would develop the three Yamato farming colonies in Merced County (Matsumoto 1993, 26–30).

Japanese who shifted their focus from the homeland as a place of return to the United States as a place of residence faced significant challenges. These challenges had largely to do with structural and practical racism against Asians. The 1790 Naturalization Act was limited to "free white persons." After the US Civil War, an amendment to the act allowed aliens of African nativity and persons of African descent to naturalize, leaving Asians as the primary racially excluded class (Smith 2002). That connection was reinforced in the Chinese Exclusion Act, which specifically noted that Chinese were "aliens ineligible for citizenship." Significant Caucasian organizations also pushed for school and labor segregation of the Japanese. This came to a head in 1906 when the school board in San Francisco moved to segregate students of Japanese ancestry from the rest of the population. By this time, estimates suggest that around 70,000 Japanese immigrants were living in the continental United States. Of these, upward of 38,000 came to the United States through Hawaii (Ichioka 1988, 51–52).

The segregation of schools was an affront to the Japanese government, which had new global clout as a result of its recent victory in the Sino-Russian War. It put significant pressure on the US federal government to persuade the San Francisco school board to change the policy. This was brokered in what came to be known as the "Gentleman's Agreement," in which the Japanese government agreed to stop issuing exit visas to the United States for laborers and President Theodore Roosevelt brokered a deal to end segregation of the San Francisco schools. The final piece was a 1907 Executive Order that effectively cut off Hawaii as a back door for Japanese immigration. This stemmed the tide, but passage remained open for those related to Japanese already in the United States. After 1907, the most common arrivals were women married to immigrant husbands either in person or remotely. One can see the effect of this immigration pattern in the 1920 US Census, by which time the population of those with Japanese ancestry in the United States was enumerated at 111,010, of which over 22,000 were married women and nearly 30,000 American-born children (Matsumoto 1993, 25).

Histories of the Japanese American community typically differentiate between the Issei, or first-generation immigrants, and the Nisei, or the second generation born in the United States. And certainly, there could be a big cultural divide between them. Issei were enculturated to subsume individual desires to family and group obligation (Ichioka 1988). Although many of them would convert to Christianity, Shinto respect for both nature and ancestors ran as a current beneath other beliefs. Issei were also, because of the law, unable to become American citizens, a status bestowed on their children at birth. Universal education meant that Japanese American children typically went to schools where they became fluent in English and interacted with non-Nikkei children. Their linguistic and intercultural skills helped the Nisei serve as brokers for their communities.

Just as some of the first generation of immigrants came to the United States for education, during the second generation, many students returned to Japan for their training. The important role these individuals played in the continuity of Japanese family connections and traditions is marked linguistically: such individuals are known as Kibei or Kibei-Nisei if they were among the second generation (Hoobler and Hoobler 1996, 91). The Kibei experienced the modernizing Japan of the early twentieth century and returned home with a different understanding of the homeland than that of their parents. They also often felt in limbo, belonging culturally to neither generation (Okihiro 2013).

Because of their legal status, Nisei would also come to play a significant role in their families' economics. Agitation over the success of Japanese Americans in agriculture became a rallying point for anti-Asian organizations and politicians. Fueled by "yellow peril" rhetoric, in 1913 California passed legislation to restrict land ownership based on citizenship status. The law made it illegal for "aliens ineligible for citizenship," primarily Asian immigrants, to buy land in the state. The law was revisited and strengthened in 1920 and 1923. Many states followed California's lead. Similar alien land laws were passed in Washington, Oregon, and Arizona. Other states like New Mexico amended their state constitutions to exclude alien land ownership. Notably, Colorado was one of the few western states that did not have such restrictions. Indeed, such a measure was defeated at the ballot in the fall of 1944 (Hosokawa 2005).

One method to bypass the alien land restrictions was for land to be purchased as gifts to, or in holding companies for, the Nisei children of Japanese families. As citizens, *Nisei* were not subject to alien land laws; however, watchdogs still contested their ownership. Some contended that such children were too young to be true landowners. However, farming in Japan had always been a deeply family-based enterprise. As soon as they were able, children were expected to contribute their labor (Fukutake 1980). This tradition continued in the United States; when contested, such children could often show that they did act as farmers on their own land. This was the case for the Fujita family of Petaluma, California, some of whom would later end up at Amache.

Tsuneji and Matsuno Fujita emigrated to the United States from Okayama, Japan, in 1905, finding work at the Spreckels Sugar Company farm near Salinas, California (Dennis Fujita, personal communication 2013). Sugar beet propagation required troops of workers for the significant "stoop" labor involved in cultivation. While in Salinas, the Fujitas had four children: two boys and two girls. In 1920, the family of six began raising chickens on 7 acres of leased land in Sonoma County. At that time, Henry (Katsumi) was twelve and his brother George (Eigi) was ten. In his family history, Henry's son Dennis writes of the boys, "Before and after school, they were expected to feed the chickens, collect eggs, clean chicken houses, administer medications to sick birds and plow the fields to raise kale as supplemental feed for the chickens" (Fujita 2011, 6). By 1923, the family had raised enough capital to purchase land, and Tsuneji and Matsuno did so as a gift to their four children. By that time, the boys were handling the majority of the ranch work, especially business dealings, because their father did not speak fluent English. So Henry and George were the ones who dealt with Caucasian suppliers, dealers, and customers.

In 1928, Tsuneji Fujita was taken to court in a suit that claimed he and his children owned land in violation of the California Alien Land Law. The California attorney general and Sonoma County district attorney contended that Fujita's children were of "tender years" and that Tsuneji was in fact the cultivator of the land and received all of the profits from it (*People v. Fujita*, 8 P.2d 1011 [Cal. 1932]). What ultimately won the suit for the Fujita family was the clear evidence that Henry and George were not only farm owners on paper but farmers in their own right. The Fujita sons also dealt with money, which was deposited into a family account. Testimony was provided not just by Henry and George but also by the Caucasians with whom they had business relationships (*People v. Fujita*). Although not admitted as evidence in court, family photographs also capture the boys at work plowing fields and building chicken houses (figure 3.1).

FIGURE 3.1. George (Eigi) Fujita plowing a field to plant kale for chickens raised on the family farm. *Courtesy,* family of Tsuneji and Matsuno Fujita.

While the West Coast of the United States was roiled by anti-Asian struggles, the East Coast faced the tide of European immigration coming through Ellis Island. Many of these immigrants came from Southern and Eastern Europe, and concerns similar to those regarding Asians were raised about them: namely, they were too unlike the majority population of the United States to be assimilated. Concern over national security after World War I was another factor driving xenophobia. With a conservative President Calvin Coolidge at the helm of the executive branch, the US Congress passed the 1924 Immigration Act, which set quotas favoring immigration of Western Europeans. It also, in violation of the Gentleman's Agreement, ended all immigration from Japan by closing the door to all aliens ineligible for citizenship.

With the end of immigration, the growth in the number of Japanese in the United States was completely a result of the increase in the numbers of Nisei and eventually Sansei (the third generation). The next two decades were characterized by the creation of stable Japanese American communities, both rural and urban (Hoobler and Hoobler 1996). Traditional practices were reinforced through organizations based on home prefecture, businesses that catered to the community, and through Japanese schools (*gakko*) attended (sometimes unwillingly) by many Nisei. Typically held after the regular school day, Japanese schools taught language, arts, and martial arts such as kendo and sumo. Yet new American-inspired traditions took hold in these communities as well, with baseball a particularly popular activity. A melding of ethnic pride and popular culture is also evidenced in events like Nisei week in Los Angeles, which included a parade and the crowning of an American-style beauty queen.

Data from the 1940 US Census indicate that on the eve of the war, there were just under 127,000 people of Japanese ancestry in the continental United States, the vast majority of whom lived along the West Coast. Over 93,000 lived in California alone, with the other Pacific Coast states making up most of the remainder (DeWitt 1943). Families and the closing of immigration had made a significant demographic impact: in 1940, nearly 64 percent of people of Japanese ancestry in the continental United States were American born and under thirty years old (DeWitt 1943). For adults, older employment patterns continued to strongly shape the community. Agriculture was by far the most dominant employment sector for West Coast Japanese Americans, with 45 percent of the population making their living in that field (DeWitt 1943). Another 26 percent were involved in agriculture-related activities (Helphand 2006) such as running produce markets or, especially in the greater Los Angeles area, working as gardeners (Hirahara 2000). Nursery owners and flower growers were another important sector of the community. Other entrepreneurs sold different goods and services, many, but not all, catering to other Japanese Americans or Asians. Professionals were often in the service of their community as doctors, ministers, and educators.

Community Portraits: Life before Amache

A sketch of several Japanese American communities in California brings life to this general historical outline. The remainder of this chapter discusses regions that would become associated with Amache. Although they existed in the shade of racism, these were vibrant communities whose history should not disappear under the cloud hindsight might cast for them.

Japantowns, or Nihonmachi, became a prominent feature of many urban centers along the West Coast. Seattle, Portland, Los Angeles, and San Francisco each had the features of such ethnic enclaves: neighborhoods containing religious institutions, Japanese-language newspapers, organizations reflecting connections in Japan, after-school programs for young people, and restaurants or markets with traditional foods. The Japantown in Los Angeles, known as Little Tokyo, is still a vibrant Nikkei cultural center for the region and the country, hosting such organizations as the Japanese American Cultural and Community Center, the Japanese American National Museum, and the Southern California Gardeners Federation.

Historically, a number of neighborhoods with relatively high populations of Japanese Americans were spread throughout the Los Angeles basin, not just in Little Tokyo. The Seinan was a multiethnic neighborhood southwest of the city center, a location reflected in its name (literally *southwest* in Japanese). As a community history notes, the social lives of the Nikkei who lived there "revolved around the churches, temples and prefectural organizations of their ancestors in Japan, and also the local public neighborhood schools, playgrounds, and parks" (Uchima and Shinmoto 2010, 7). It was largely through their children that the residents of different ethnic backgrounds—Japanese American, African American, Latino, and some Caucasians—built social bonds.

This mix of ethnicities was no accident. The Seinan was the by-product of restrictive racial and ethnic housing covenants in other Los Angeles neighborhoods. Here, people of color could lease or purchase houses and businesses. By 1940, over 3,000 Nikkei were living in the neighborhood, with three different religious institutions serving them: two that were Christian and one Buddhist temple (Uchima and Shinmoto 2010). Prominent Japanese businesses in the neighborhood included a number of nurseries, retail stores, and a cleaners and dye works. The Fujisaka drug store employed a pharmacist, and other Japanese healthcare professionals served the local population, including a dentist and a doctor.

The neighborhood's location on the edge of town was a boon for truck farmers and those in other agricultural industries, such as the Los Angeles wholesale produce market. Two prominent nurseries were located in the Seinan. Both the Iba and the Western Avenue Park Nurseries were family affairs, nestled in residential areas. Many Japanese families in the neighborhood also had "backyard nurseries" (Uchima and Shinmoto 2010). Alice Fukuda Tanaka grew up in Seinan and kindly discussed her family's experience with me. Her father, Louis Goro Fukuda, was a truck farmer and produce merchant specializing in celery, like many in the area. He forged a bond with his Scottish immigrant neighbor, Mr. Campbell, who also grew celery (Tanaka 2011).

The Nisei children of the neighborhood participated in American organizations and pastimes, like Boy Scouts and baseball. But they also attended Japanese schools and played sports like kendo and judo. Once they completed high school, the Nisei residents of the neighborhood often attended nearby University of Southern California or the University of California, Los Angeles (UCLA). Sho Iino's life history follows this arc. Born in Berkeley, Ino and his family moved to the Seinan where he attended Manual Arts High School. He was the first Japanese American named to the All Los Angeles City B Basketball team. After graduation, he enrolled at UCLA, majoring in accounting (Uchima and Shinmoto 2010).[1]

Other tight-knit communities were found in rural areas. The first of the three Yamato Colonies was formed just outside Livingston, California. An advertisement for the colony land reflected Kyutaro Abiko's philosophy: "We believe that the Japanese must settle permanently with their countrymen on large pieces of land if they are to succeed in America" (cited in Noda 1981, 10). The first settlers, who arrived in 1906, were promised that after a small payment, their profit would easily cover later payments. For the most part this was true; however, the claim that the soil was rich and suitable for all crops was less so. Located in the Central Valley of California, the surface soils were very sandy and underlain by hardpan clay. Early residents recall fighting dust storms and hordes of rabbits, as well as a distinct lack of shade. The *San Francisco Chronicle* described the first colony as having been "blown away" (Noda 1981, 19).

The Yamato locale did have several advantages, including existing irrigation and proximity to a railroad line, which linked it to important markets in both San Francisco and Los Angeles. Founded before the passing of California's alien land law, Yamato drew both single men and families, including several of the project's financial backers, which likely deepened their commitment to the colony's success (Noda 1981, 13). Settlers with key practical skills like

---

1   Like many Nisei professionals, Ino had to fight for acceptance. After World War II, he gained entrance as a certified public accountant in the Midwest. His Ohio certification allowed him to move back to California to start his own accounting firm (Minoru Tonai, personal communication 2018).

civil engineering and those with training in agriculture were also assets. In addition, many of the settlers were longtime residents of the United States, another factor that helped residents negotiate the many social and economic challenges of land development. Residents helped one another, such as the Minabe family, who owned a two-story home near the colony and took in many early colonists as boarders while they built their own homes (Noda 1981). Settlers often worked together to build housing and dig wells. Many chose to plant grape vines or orchards; while those matured, they raised other cash crops such as sweet potatoes, tomatoes, and melons. With investments that would take years to recoup, income was often minimal, and many colonists relied on outside sources like seasonal agricultural labor to make ends meet. By its first decade, the community had been solidified through a farming cooperative, the construction of a community hall, and the establishment of a Christian church (Noda 1981).

In the late 1910s, the original Yamato colonists were joined by settlers who established two other Yamato Colonies: Cressey and Cortez. The original settlers of the Yamato Colony clustered nearer the town of Livingston (and would soon take on that name), while the newer residents bought plots within that original filing but nearer the town of Cressey (figure 3.2). Cortez, located nearer the town of Turlock, was a new development and physically separated from the others. The residents in these new settlements faced many of the same struggles as the earlier colonists but also an additional legal one: the alien land laws. Most of the residents of the new colonies purchased their land for their Nisei children. Their arrival strained established relationships between the residents of Yamato and their Caucasian neighbors. The subversion of the intent of the alien land laws was one reason, but another was the apparent class differences: while many professionals had been involved in the first colony, Cressey and Cortez settlers were largely working class (Matsumoto 1993; Noda 1981). They were also less likely to be Christian; it was in Cortez that the first Buddhist temple in the Yamato Colonies was established.

The newer arrivals also had less of a cushion when the region was hit hard by the Great Depression. Prices for produce dropped significantly, and outside sources of income were not as easy to find. As Valerie J. Matsumoto (1993, 47) writes in her history of Cortez, it was through the development of economic, religious, and educational institutions that the town was able to

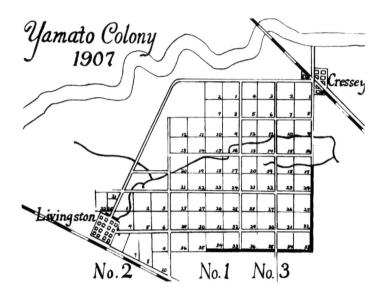

FIGURE 3.2. Historical plat map of the Yamato Colony. Original available at the Merced County Clerk Recorder/Assessors Office, Merced, CA.

survive and even thrive. The one institution that was vital for every resident was the Cortez Growers Association, which allowed for collective power in shipping, marketing, and purchasing. The association's first full-time manager was Sam Kuwahara, who as a Nisei was fluent in English and a citizen. Many other communal enterprises not only brought people together, they laid the physical groundwork for the community. A great example is the kabuki-style play put on as a fundraiser by the membership of the Cortez Presbyterian Church in a railway shed behind the Growers Association offices (Matsumoto 1993, 52–53).

Not all Japanese Americans in California lived in ethnic enclaves. This was certainly the case for the northern Central Valley and the coast. There were some pockets of Japanese residents, including in Petaluma. Like the poultry-raising Fujita family, many Nikkei in the area raised eggs and chickens destined for San Francisco markets, while others tended fruit orchards or were truck farmers (Nakano 2016). Some families moved seasonally from the hop fields north of Sacramento to coastal farms to pick crops like grapes. Others, like the two Nikkei families in Sausalito (Hirano 2014), were dispersed among largely non-Japanese neighbors.

A critical node in the dispersed coastal Nikkei community was the Enmanji Buddhist Temple in Sebastapol. Housed in a striking medieval-style Japanese temple building, it was founded in 1926 as a Buddhist Sunday School and Japanese-language school. The Buddhist mission acquired the current building from the 1933 Chicago World's Fair and relocated it by train to its current site (Enmanji Buddhist Temple 2016). The Sonoma County chapter of the Japanese American Citizens League was founded just one year later. Although the chapter struggled with funding and membership at first, it grew into an important organization for both Issei and Nisei residents of the area (Nakano 2016).

American Nikkei and the Japanese Gardening Tradition

Visitors to the Enmanji Buddhist Temple today encounter stone lanterns and precisely pruned trees flanking the front entrance. Such Japanese-style garden elements are now common in Nikkei public buildings. But historical photographs of the Enmanji temple suggest that this landscaping was not in existence before the war. Indeed, the extent to which such gardens were a common part of people's pre-war lives has not been the subject of much research. Luckily, there are some resources for beginning to explore the question.

In the course of research for this book, I surveyed over 1,000 photographs taken during the 1930s by California Nikkei. They are available online through the California State University (CSU) Japanese American Digitization Project (https://calisphere.org/collections/26203/). What these 1930s images suggest is that for the most part, community buildings such as Buddhist temples, Japanese schools, and community halls had little landscaping, and only in a few instances did that landscaping contain elements we often associate with Japanese-style gardens. With a few very interesting exceptions (figure 3.3), this type of landscaping also does not seem prominent in Nikkei front yards or backyards.

Yet Japanese-style gardens are not uncommon in community photographs. Many document family visits to exposition gardens, including those built on Treasure Island for the Golden Gate International Exposition in 1939 (figure

FIGURE 3.3. Traditional house and landscape at Terminal Island, California, 1930s. Reprinted with permission from the Gerth Archives and Special Collections, CSU Dominguez Hills.

FIGURE 3.4. Japanese Americans visiting the World's Fair garden on Treasure Island, California, 1939. Reprinted with permission from the Gerth Archives and Special Collections, CSU Dominguez Hills.

FIGURE 3.5. A Kibei visits a formal garden in Japan with her school group, 1930s. *Courtesy*, CSU Fullerton Pollak Library, University Archives and Special Collections, Japanese American Internment in California.

3.4). Oral histories also suggest that visits to such gardens were common practice: the Nisei parents of one of our Amache volunteers visited the Japanese garden at Golden Gate Park on their honeymoon (Anita Miyamoto Miller, personal communication 2018).

Another interesting twist on the relationship of these communities to Japanese gardens is also evidenced in this photographic collection. Gardens are prominent in photographs taken in Japan, whether by people visiting their families or by Kibei, who can be seen posing in gardens with their classmates (figure 3.5). The CSU digital collection highlights how the transnational nature of these communities meant that the connection to Japanese-style gardens happened throughout the diaspora. The photographic evidence also aligns with scholarship on how gardens in Japan became potent symbols and tourist attractions in the late nineteenth and early twentieth centuries (Tagsold 2017).

The symbolic work of Japanese-style gardens in the United States is featured in the scholarship of Kendall H. Brown. He notes that these spaces were "a crucial part of the immigrant experience for many ethnic Japanese in the West, integral in terms of economics and the politics of identity" (Brown 1999, 12). For example, Nikkei were somehow involved, whether as designers, laborers, or sponsors, with almost all of the Japanese-style gardens in North America. These include many of the World's Fair or exposition gardens built in the United States, like the gardens surrounding the Enmanji temple building when it was in Chicago. Other fairs that featured Japanese gardens were those in St. Louis (1904) and San Diego (1915) (Brown 2013). Some of these exposition gardens continued their lives as commercial enterprises, as with the Golden Gate tea garden in San Francisco. Other commercial gardens included those associated with nurseries and Japanese restaurants. Some private gardens built for prominent Nikkei were occasionally available to the community. For instance, the Los Angeles Fukunaga family garden served as the backdrop for pre-war Nisei week events (Brown 1999, 13). A few permanent public gardens were built by Nikkei, including school gardens built by parents in Sierra Madre, Los Angeles, and Redwood City, California. Oral histories also tell of smaller, lesser-known gardens at schools in Compton or built by Issei for their own families, business associates, and friends (Minoru Tonai, personal communication 2018).

Evidence suggests that members of the pre-World War II Nikkei community might not have engaged with Japanese-style gardens or landscaping on a daily basis, especially those living in more rural settings. Yet many, perhaps most, would have had at least some experience with such landscapes ranging from designing or maintaining them to visiting them, both in the United States and Japan. Perhaps more important, the values expressed in Japanese gardens, especially respect for nature and its beauty, were woven through many aspects of the community, whether through worship, work, or leisure activities.

In chapter 4, readers will follow these diasporic communities, with their trans-Pacific ties, to a most unlikely spot: the High Plains of Colorado. Although they were far from the lush archipelago, values and skills from their ancestral home, as well as from their new communities in America, came with them.

4

A Prison on the Prairie

In 2014, archaeology crews at Amache were excavating in an area of the site slated for the reconstruction of several structures. One, a replica guard tower, had already been completed, with a barrack soon to follow. We were visited by a group of young children, mostly elementary school age, from a local summer school program. When working with kids, it is important to tailor our message and to keep them safe around open test excavations, so we always have designated tour guides for school groups.

That day our guides included former incarceree Anita Miyamoto Miller. Anita was a very young girl at Amache and doesn't remember much of her time there. One reason she recalls little is that her older relatives refused to talk about the camp. But Anita is determined that the generational silence ends with her. Working on the archaeology at Amache has been a way for her to learn more about her own and her family's experience and to share it with her children and grandchildren.

Selecting Anita to help lead the tour group was an obvious choice. She could both address the archaeology we were doing and speak to children

DOI: 10.5876/9781646420933.c004

about her experience as a child at Amache. In an unforgettable moment, one of the kids asked Anita, "Why did they put you in here?" Standing in the shadow of the reconstructed guard tower, she answered honestly, "I don't know. I think they were afraid of us."

Just like the guard tower's, the shadows of internment are constantly cast on Amache. It is the end product of the systematic targeting, removal, and incarceration of legal residents and US citizens based on their ethnicity. Without understanding that history, little at the site makes sense. But framed in that context, the site bears witness to an often unspeakable moment of the American past.

Many masterful books have been written about how the Japanese in America were caught up by the tides of World War II (e.g., Daniels 1972; Robinson 2010; Weglyn 1996), and a number of them are cited here. Particularly important and freely accessible online is *Personal Justice Denied*, the report of the Commission on Wartime Relocation and Internment of Civilians (CWRIC) (1992). Composed of a group of scholars appointed by the US Congress to investigate the removal and incarceration of Japanese Americans during World War II, the CWRIC was instrumental in widespread recognition of, in its terms, the "grave injustice" of the internment. This chapter begins with a brief overview of the nationwide process of removal and incarceration but then focuses on how it played out at Amache.

The Big Roundup

World War II had been raging in Europe for several years when the Japanese Imperial Navy made a preemptive attack on the American fleet stationed in Pearl Harbor, Hawaii, on December 7, 1941. To many Americans, the act confirmed their fears of the "yellow peril" (Wei 2016). Indeed, in a country saturated with anti-Asian sentiment, the reaction to the bombing of Pearl Harbor was predictable. As scholar Roger Daniels (1993, 3) trenchantly writes, "The wartime abuse of Japanese Americans, it is now clear, was merely a link in a chain of racism that stretched back to the earliest contacts between Asians and whites on American soil."

Nikkei who lived through this moment remember vividly their apprehension and fear. Atsushi Kikuchi, who was living in Los Angeles, recalled, "I went to church on the streetcar and everybody was glaring at me. I couldn't figure out why. It never happened before. So then I went to church and they said Pearl Harbor was attacked" (cited in Gesensway and Roseman 1987, 135). Others remember the authorities coming for their fathers, not knowing where they had been taken or for how long (Minoru Tonai, personal communication 2018). Newspaper publishers, businessmen with ties to Japan, Buddhist and Shinto priests, and Japanese veterans were classified as "suspicious persons." These individuals, many of whom were community leaders, were rounded up immediately after Pearl Harbor, and most were eventually sent to prison camps run by the US Department of Justice.

The target was not confined to individuals. Concerned by fishermen and cannery workers' access to boats and the short-wave radios needed to operate them safely, the United States Navy ordered all Nikkei living on Terminal Island, California, to leave in early February, with no provision for where they should go (Daniels 1993). Originally given a month, the residents were shocked when on February 25 they saw notices to vacate the island by midnight on the 27th. The panic to leave was exacerbated by the fact that many heads of households had been among those arrested immediately following Pearl Harbor (Okihiro 2013, 42).

Further inland, police searched homes for items that had been deemed contraband for Japanese American ownership, including weapons and radios. In addition, the assets of all Issei, who were now considered "enemy aliens," were frozen, as were all accounts in American branches of Japanese banks (Burton et al. 2002). This left the Japanese American community hobbled through both economic hardship and the loss of many leaders.

And what were they facing? Loud voices—union leaders, newspaper publishers, and local politicians—stirring smoldering resentment into a full flame of paranoia. Certainly, concerns about the safety of the country were legitimate, especially on the West Coast. Yet the fear that Nikkei would serve as spies—or worse, terrorists—in the cause of their homeland was radically unfounded. Intelligence reports by both the FBI and the United States Navy suggested that the Japanese in the United States posed no military threat. Indeed, one report noted that the Issei were for the most part loyal to their new country, and the Nisei were distrusted by those in Japan (CWRIC 1992, 52–53). Yet the claim of military necessity continued to be made, often by those who would profit the most from exiling the Nikkei from their West Coast homes.

The person often singled out as the critical fulcrum point in this history is General John DeWitt, who oversaw the West Coast for the US Department of War. DeWitt believed the Japanese were inherently "an enemy race" and that even the third generation, or Sansei, could turn against their nation (CWRIC 1992, 82). He actually used the lack of any anti-government activity on the part of the Japanese in the United States as evidence against them. He claimed that "the very fact that no sabotage has taken place to date is a disturbing and confirming indication that such action will be taken" (CWRIC 1992, 82). DeWitt was not alone; the majority of federal and local government officials either supported or did not protest the targeting of Japanese Americans. Most important among them was the president of the United States.

On February 19, 1942, ten weeks after the Japanese attack on Pearl Harbor, President Franklin D. Roosevelt signed Executive Order 9066. This act gave the secretary of war the authority to exclude from strategic areas any persons (citizens or not) identified as possible threats to security. Although it did not specifically mention people of Japanese heritage, it was clearly designed to pave the way for the removal of Nikkei from the West Coast of the United States. Within weeks, the Western Defense Command had drawn the boundaries of exclusion zones along the coast. Military Area no. 1 included the western half of Washington, Oregon, and California and the southern half of Arizona, while Military Area no. 2 included the remainder of those states. Within that area lived the vast majority of the Japanese in the US mainland (figure 4.1). The military was able to access the locations of Japanese Americans using block-by-block census data that are typically protected by law but were made available under provisions of the Second War Powers Act of 1942 (CWRIC 1992; Minkel 2007).

As many have noted (e.g., Nagata 1993), if security was truly the reason for internment, the Japanese in Hawaii would have been similarly targeted. Yet the one place where the Japanese had struck the United States and where (unfounded) accounts of possible Japanese American espionage existed was not designated an exclusion zone. At the time, Japanese Americans comprised nearly a third of the territory's population. Their exclusion would have collapsed the Hawaiian economy and social structure. There was also, importantly, significantly less call for such a move by Hawaiian politicians and authorities. Although community leaders were also imprisoned there during the war, only 1 percent of Hawaii's Nikkei population would be interned

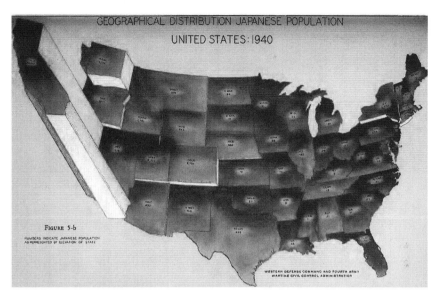

FIGURE 4.1. Map of Japanese American populations by state prior to World War II. DeWitt 1943, figure 5-B. Government document.

(Nagata 1993, 3). Residents were under numerous restrictions, however, ones that impinged significantly on their lives.

Nikkei on the mainland feared that widespread displacement would become a reality, and United States Army press releases regarding Military Area no. 1 suggested that their fears were not unfounded (Daniels 1972, 84). For a time, they could voluntarily leave the region. But many did not have the economic means to do so, while others were tied down by family obligations, such as caring for elderly or infirm relatives. Some families moved to live with other relatives further inland; unfortunately, many moved into Military Area no. 2, which in California was later included in the evacuation orders. Others moved further into the interior, including to Colorado.

The Japanese Americans who moved to Colorado during this time joined a population that had started to trickle into the state in the late 1800s as railroad workers and miners. Some of those immigrants stayed to farm, primarily in three regions: the San Luis Valley, the Arkansas River Valley, and the High Plains, especially clustered near the towns of Brighton, Greeley, and Fort Lupton. A small Japantown in downtown Denver served all of those communities, as well as Japanese businessmen and merchants living in the state's capital. In 2016, the Denver Buddhist Temple celebrated its 100th anniversary, and members of the *sanghas* (Buddhist congregations) from many of those farming communities were present.

The Japanese American population of other interior Western states like Utah and Idaho was somewhat similar in history and size to that in Colorado. However, voluntarily relocating to Colorado was more desirable for one particular reason: its governor, Ralph Carr, was a staunch defender of the constitutional rights of all Americans. Ten days after FDR signed Executive Order 9066, Carr gave a radio address stating that Colorado would be willing to shelter law-abiding individuals from the exclusion zones no matter their ancestry: "They are as loyal to American institutions as you and I. Many of them have been born here—are American citizens with no connection with or feeling of loyalty toward the customs and philosophies of Italy, Germany, and Japan" (cited in Hosokawa 2005, 87). Portions of the speech were published in Japanese-language newspapers, often leading those who could leave to choose Colorado as a destination. Indeed, Colorado's Japanese American population nearly doubled between Pearl Harbor and the end of "voluntary evacuation" (Schrager 2008). Among those whose moves were tracked by the military, the greatest number of Nikkei moved to Colorado (1,963), with Utah second (1,519) (CWRIC 1992, 103).

The voluntary movement of Japanese Americans away from the coasts was described trenchantly by the CWRIC (1992, 93): "From a military standpoint, this policy was bizarre and utterly impractical besides. If the *Issei* and *Nisei* were being excluded because they threatened sabotage and espionage, it is difficult to understand why they would be left at large in the interior." The overall demographic impact on the exclusion areas was also minimal—fewer than 10,000 Japanese Americans could leave on their own (Daniels 1986). Thus the Department of War set into motion a mandated (and orchestrated) removal and confinement of Japanese Americans. It did so with the support of the US Congress, which quickly passed legislation to impose criminal penalties on those who violated military orders, with little concern for the civil liberties of those involved (CWRIC 1992).

Even before the passage of that legislation, the Department of War had begun scouting sites for the confinement of Nikkei. It was to be largely a two-stage process, with temporary assembly centers to hold the population while more permanent relocation centers were constructed. Two sites—Manzanar and Poston—served as both (Daniels 1972). The military was to oversee the evacuation, but it did not want to be in the business of confining people for an unknown period of time. Thus the War Relocation Authority (WRA), a civilian administration, was born.

One of the WRA's first acts was to summon, in early April 1942, a meeting of western governors to discuss housing displaced Japanese Americans in their states. Ralph Carr's supportive position was in stark contrast to the others, especially that of Wyoming governor Nels Smith who threatened, "If you bring Japanese into my state, I promise they will be hanging from every tree" (cited in Hosokawa 2005, 90). What became clear is that—with the exception of Carr, who believed American citizens should not be held in "concentration camps" (cited in Schrager 2008, 205)—these governors would only accept Nikkei from the West Coast if they were kept under guard. This was the final straw that meant the majority of Japanese Americans would spend the war not in planned communities of the type overseen by the Farm Securities Administration during the Great Depression but in guarded facilities (Daniels 1972).

In order to proceed with removal, Military Area no. 1 was divided into over 100 evacuation areas, and the order in which they were to be taken was kept under wraps (CWRIC 1992). So although they knew it was only a matter of time, the Nikkei residents of the region had little advance notice of the actual date of their removal. Military personnel oversaw the process, which involved the posting of evacuation notices that detailed where those of Japanese ancestry (both alien and "non-alien") within the stipulated boundaries were to report and when, typically a week after the first notices were posted. Posters also noted what items "evacuees" should bring with them, including bedding, toilet articles, clothing, and eating utensils. More detailed instructions made it clear that only what could be physically carried by a family was allowed.

What had been a difficult process of selling or storing goods begun by many families in the days after Pearl Harbor became a mad rush. In fact, the significant property loss attendant to "evacuation" concerned a number of administrators. The first two removals, from Terminal Island and Bainbridge Island, Washington, had made it clear that the disposition of items was a significant problem (CWRIC 1992). Eventually, the WRA set up warehouses and

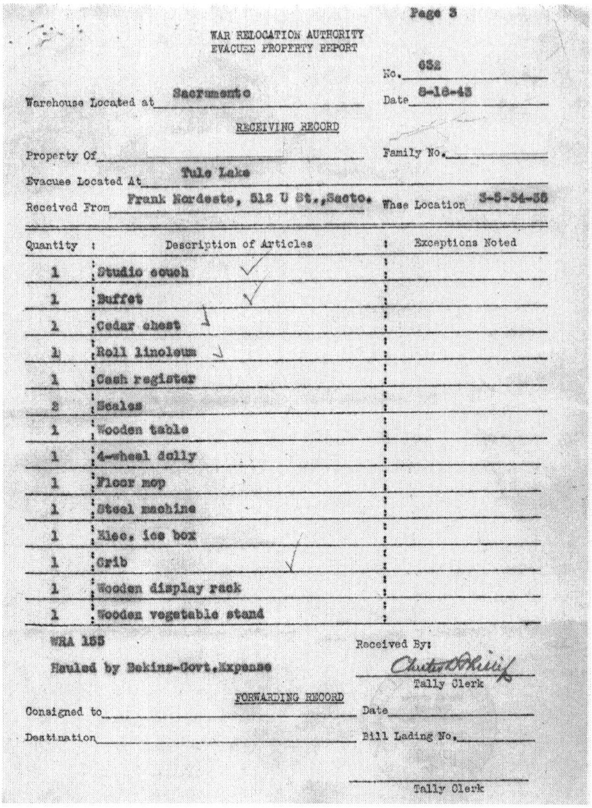

Page 3

WAR RELOCATION AUTHORITY
EVACUEE PROPERTY REPORT

No. 632

Warehouse Located at Sacramento   Date 8-18-43

RECEIVING RECORD

Property Of   Family No.

Evacuee Located At Tule Lake

Received From Frank Nordeste, 512 U St., Sacto.   Whse Location 3-5-34-35

Quantity	Description of Articles	Exceptions Noted
1	Studio couch	
1	Buffet	
1	Cedar chest	
1	Roll linoleum	
1	Cash register	
2	Scales	
1	Wooden table	
1	4-wheel dolly	
1	Floor mop	
1	Steel machine	
1	Elec. ice box	
1	Crib	
1	Wooden display rack	
1	Wooden vegetable stand	

WRA 155   Received By:

Hauled by Bekins-Govt. Expense   Tally Clerk

FORWARDING RECORD

Consigned to   Date

Destination   Bill Lading No.

Tally Clerk

FIGURE 4.2. Example inventory of items stored with the WRA by a Japanese American family. Note the combination of household items and those related to the family produce business. Courtesy, DU Amache Project.

a system for keeping track of what was in them. A page from one family's WRA inventory helps us understand what had been lost by those families not so fortunate in the timing of their removal (figure 4.2). Many farm families stored their goods in outbuildings on their property, only to discover that the subsequent tenants had little respect for their property rights, like the Cortez farmer whose family stove was seen by a Caucasian neighbor "on the road to Oklahoma" (Matsumoto 1993, 102). Especially in urban areas, families used community buildings like churches, which was a somewhat more successful strategy as long as the buildings weren't vandalized or broken into. Many families and individuals either sold items at a significant loss or just abandoned their goods.

The fact that Nikkei could only bring what they could carry when they were removed from their homes has often been seen as a symbol of political disregard for this population. The decision of what to bring and what to leave behind was traumatic for many of those removed (Uchida 1982). Photographs of families waiting in line with their few worldly goods were among those censored by the US government (Lange 2006). Oral histories suggest that the contents of those suitcases were often very pragmatic, with an emphasis on clothes and shoes. Yet when asked about what people brought to camp, former Amache incarceree Joy Takeyama Hashimoto recalled, "People were buying pie pans and tin cups, and cheap tin or aluminum silverware. But my mother said, 'My family is not going to eat off this kind of a thing.' And she took her china and her silverware" (in Foxhoven 1998).

At the designated assembly point for their "evacuation area," families were given a number that would identify them throughout their entire WRA experience. Tags with that number marked both luggage and people throughout the removal process. This reduction of personal identity to a number is a control technique common in sites of institutional confinement (Casella 2007). It was a destabilizing act, something highlighted by current artists who in their works reflect on the dehumanization of losing one's name to a number (e.g., Havey 2016).

From the assembly point, most families boarded buses to be taken to their regional "assembly centers." Meant from the outset to be temporary holding facilities while the more permanent camps were constructed, these centers had been prepared in great haste. The majority of these facilities were not meant to house people, and few met the military's standards for housing (Daniels 1972). Staying in smelly stables at a fairground or racetrack was another blow to dignity.

Patterns that would mark the internment experience were set at the assembly centers. Food was poor, unfamiliar, and served in shifts. Bathrooms were modeled on military latrines, with no stalls for privacy between either toilets or showers. Likewise, few provisions had been made for children, including appropriate food and highchairs or cribs (Daniels 1972). There were also no dietary provisions for those with particular health-related needs, such as diabetics (Minoru Tonai, personal communication 2018). Waiting in line—whether for the latrines, meals, or showers—became a prominent part of daily life. Oral histories of the Merced Assembly Center indicate that life there was "crowded, noisy, and uncomfortable" (Matsumoto 1993, 105). The centers were sites of incarceration, enclosed in fences and guarded by armed Military Police in towers. The fact that these privations were happening sometimes miles from people's homes made the situation even more difficult to comprehend. As one former incarceree recalled of her barrack at Santa Anita, "There was civilization just out there" (Fujie Hori, personal communication 2016).

In these difficult conditions, those incarcerated in the assembly centers set about creating something that more strongly resembled their lives back home. They quickly set up schools and produced newspapers, an important way for people to get information about life both inside and outside camp. Social events included talent shows, athletic events, and dances. Although it was clear that these facilities were to be very temporary, many incarcerees began to garden. Photographs of the assembly centers show vegetable or "victory" gardens next to barracks buildings, despite the very good chance that no one would be around to harvest them. At Santa Anita, some incarcerees who didn't have open ground near their barracks planted in cast-off food cans from the mess hall (Minoru Tonai, personal communication 2018).

Incarcerees also built public-area gardens at assembly centers, including a strolling garden complete with a lake in what had been the center field of the Tanforan racetrack. Artist Mine Okubo wrote about that transformation in her journal: "The lake was a great joy to the residents and presented new material for artists. In the morning sunlight and at sunset it added great beauty to the bleak barracks." Another incarceree noted that it "looks like old Japan" (both cited in Helphand 2006, 159).

After three to six months, incarcerees at all of the facilities except Manzanar and Poston were displaced again, this time to the additional eight purpose-built camps in the interior (figure 4.3). Once again packing up their few worldly belongings, incarcerees boarded trains for a long ride to the interior. Not told where they were going or how long it would take, the ride was both uncomfortable and unnerving. As specified by the US Department of War, all ten WRA camps were built in locations distant from population centers and munitions plants. Locations were also determined by existing rail lines, which were critical for bringing in both goods and people. The

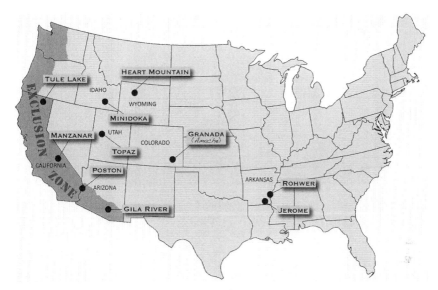

FIGURE 4.3. Map of all ten WRA camps and exclusion zone. *Courtesy*, Anne Amati.

WRA's intent was to house the incarcerees in locations where their agricultural skills could be put to good use, both to offset the cost of their confinement and also to make lands in the public domain more productive (Chiang 2010). Largely undeveloped, the camps tended to be less than ideal locales for occupation—many were considered downright desolate.

Amache: A Prison on the Prairie

The Granada Relocation Center, better known by its postal designation, Amache, was located 1½ miles outside the small town of Granada in southeastern Colorado. Before the war, Granada was just one of the small farming towns that dotted the valley of the Arkansas River, which runs east a few miles north of the site. Lamar, the Prowers County seat and largest town in the county, is 17 miles west.[1] Geographically, Amache is located in the High Plains, a semiarid region between the Rocky Mountains and the Great Plains. Summers are hot and dry, with occasional severe thunderstorms and

---

1   According to the US Census, in 1940 the population of Granada was 342, while Lamar had 1,475 residents.

tornadoes. Winters are generally cold and dry but can bring heavy snowfall. Low humidity and high wind are common throughout the year and can combine to create choking dust storms (Clark and Scheiber 2008).

Despite the region's general aridity, the Arkansas River provided irrigation water for the fields along the bottomland of the valley where the soil was more suitable for agriculture. The Arkansas Valley was served by the Atchison, Topeka, and Santa Fe Railroad and US Highway 50, both of which linked it to national transportation networks. Granada was founded in the late 1800s as a railroad town but quickly transitioned to largely agricultural enterprises. The town and the region were tremendously hard hit by the Great Depression and the Dust Bowl. It remained an economically depressed area until World War II.

Amache was the only incarceration camp where the land was in private ownership prior to the war. The entire project area was over 10,000 acres, the majority of which was earmarked for the camp's agricultural program. It was composed primarily of two previously existing facilities, the Koen Ranch and the X-Y Ranch. Both parcels held mixed agricultural enterprises with existing irrigation and farm structures, including a working dairy farm. To create a consolidated area, another twelve small agricultural holdings were also included in the project area. Only one property owner was a willing seller, and the majority of the land had to be taken through condemnation, an action that set a combative tone between the WRA and the local residents (Harvey 2003, 61).

The primary area of the camp was a 1-square-mile parcel sited above the valley floor, on sandy lands previously used minimally for livestock grazing. Developed along the blueprint of all the WRA camps (figure 4.4), the central camp area housed the WRA administration, MPs, and inmates. These "forced communities" followed a hybrid template of US military outposts and Depression-era federal experiments in planned towns built for migrant farm workers (Horiuchi 2005). Encircled by barbed wire fences and guard towers, the camp was gridded out with a series of streets given numeric or alphabetical designation. Areas devoted to camp administration (including housing) were located in the northwest quadrant of the camp. In the northeast were Military Police housing, the camp's motor pool, and the hospital. The remainder to the south, about two thirds of the camp, was devoted to blocks housing the incarcerees. In the center were public blocks for the high school, its

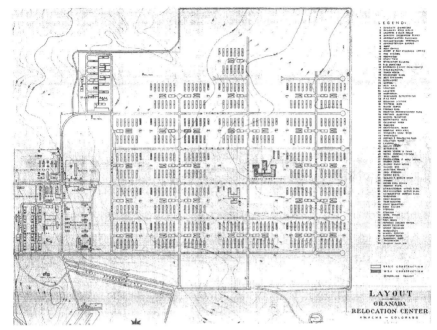

FIGURE 4.4. Historical map of central area of Amache. Map oriented with east at the top. Government document in author's possession.

playing fields, community services like the police headquarters (and later the incarceree-run cooperative), and one block that would remain undeveloped. In the area west of the fence were support facilities, such as the root cellar and coal storage, as well as the camp cemetery. The sewage settling ponds were close enough that former incarcerees remember the severe smell during strong northwesterly winds (Minoru Tonai, personal communication 2018).

Barracks blocks were identical, although oriented north or south depending on the location of developed roads (figure 4.5). Centered in the block and adjacent to the road was the mess hall. Behind this stood an H-shaped building that was a combination latrine, shower, and laundry. Twelve barracks buildings, each 120 feet long and 20 feet wide, flanked these shared facilities. The barracks were divided into six living units: at the end were the smallest, which were 16 feet long and held two–three people. They shared an entrance with the largest units in each building, which were 24 feet long and typically set aside for families of six–seven people. In the center was a pair of square

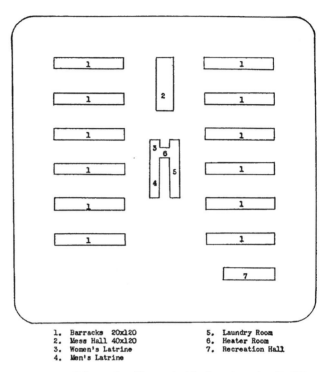

1. Barracks 20x120
2. Mess Hall 40x120
3. Women's Latrine
4. Men's Latrine
5. Laundry Room
6. Heater Room
7. Recreation Hall

FIGURE 4.5. Schematic of barracks block at Amache. DeWitt 1943. figure 23. Government document.

units, 20 feet by 20 feet. Rooms typically held families but could also include unrelated individuals to fill the room to capacity. Each block also had a 100 foot by 20 foot recreation hall (stenciled "Rec Hall" on the outside). However, in many instances they were used to house organizations such as churches, youth groups, and, in Block 6H, the headquarters for all the block managers.

All of these buildings were hastily constructed by crews with little experience. They were modified theater of war buildings built of green wood protected from the elements only by asphalt rolled roofing on the outside and (eventually) thin insulation boards on the inside. Unfortunately, there are few good images of the interior of the barracks, likely because of their poor lighting, which consisted of windows and a single bare bulb. What images we do have were staged by the WRA, which chose very specific subjects and supplemented the poor interior lighting. So although we should not

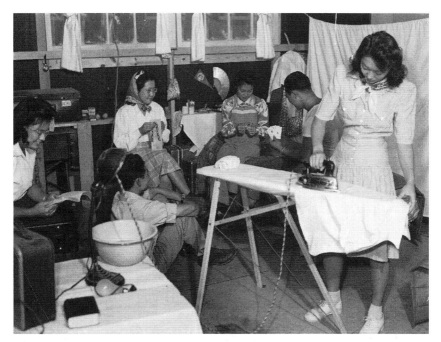

FIGURE 4.6. WRA photograph of the interior of an Amache barracks building taken soon after occupation. Photograph by Tom Parker, chief photographer of the WRA. Government document available on Calisphere.

interpret them as a true slice of camp life, the images do highlight key features of the Amache living units (figure 4.6). Most of them had crude brick floors laid directly into the sandy native soil. Rooms were heated by a single coal-burning stove. The only furniture items provided to incarcerees were army cots and thin cotton mattresses. There were no internal walls within units, but improvised dividers like blankets were used to separate living and sleeping areas (a tactic visible in figure 4.6). As one former Amache incarceree recalled, "It was one room per family and the living was cramped at best. Everything was made of flimsy clapboard that looked like it would collapse at any moment" (Lurie 1982, 38). As the green wood dried, exterior wall gaps formed, allowing dust and snow to blow into the rooms. Archaeology crews often encounter evidence of how incarcerees combated this situation. They find homemade buckets filled with tar for patching walls and concrete lips that would have filled gaps between the foundation and barrack walls.

FIGURE 4.7. Map of the census districts in California whose Japanese American populations were sent to Amache. Image based on a historical US Department of War map. *Courtesy*, Anne Amati.

The original Amache population came from three main geographic areas, all in California: the Central Valley, the northern coast, and southwest Los Angeles (figure 4.7). The first to arrive at Amache on August 27, 1942, was a group of 212 incarcerees from the Merced Assembly Center who had volunteered to help complete camp construction. They found that many basic resources, like showers, flush toilets, and the mess halls, were not functional (Noda 1981). The benefit of early arrival, though slight, was greater access to construction materials with which they could fashion furniture or make structural changes to the barracks (Noda 1981). Within a few weeks, they were joined by the remaining population of the Merced Assembly Center. On September 19, the first trainload of incarcerees from the Santa Anita Assembly Center arrived, with more following throughout the month. Neighbors and friends gathered together when assigned to barracks, which helped reconstitute connections frayed by removal and also contributed to the character of different areas of the camp (Kamp-Whittaker and Clark 2019).

By the end of September 1942, there were 7,434 prisoners at Amache from those two assembly centers. Although it was the smallest of the ten WRA camps, Amache was suddenly the tenth largest city in Colorado (Simmons and Simmons 2004). In time, this original group would be joined by inmates transferred from other WRA facilities, including over 900 from Tule Lake and over 500 from Jerome. Other transfers included those released from US Department of Justice camps and individuals who petitioned to be with their family at Amache. All told, over 10,000 people spent at least part of the war at Amache. They hailed almost evenly from rural and urban areas, and both Buddhist and Christian denominations were well represented in the camp. Most of the formerly rural residents were farming families, especially from Livingston, Cressey, and Cortez (the Yamato Colonies in California). Urban populations included truck farmers, gardeners, and merchants. The hospital was staffed by Nikkei doctors, nurses, pharmacists, and a dentist. Other notable professionals in the camp were two professors, two cartoonists from the Walt Disney studios, a concert singer, and several lawyers.

Echoing their activities at assembly centers, the Nikkei in Amache worked quickly to transform the military facility into a town. They accomplished this through many avenues: the creation of a community council with a representative from each block, the organization of churches and social groups, sporting activities, and improvement of the physical facilities. Some efforts, like the camp newspaper, were supported by funds and staffing from the War Relocation Authority. Others, including the constant cycle of social events, were incarceree-driven, including the first social and dance, which was held within weeks of the camp's opening. It was organized by the early arrivals for the first trainload of their compatriots from the Merced Assembly Center (WRA 1945).

Arts and crafts held a central role in camp life. The fluorescence of art in all ten of the incarceration camps has been the subject of multiple studies and exhibits, beginning in the decade following the camps. Art historian Allen H. Eaton (1952) enthusiastically extolled the quality and sheer mass of art produced by incarcerees. Some of the forms of craft he described were new to most in the Japanese American community, such as weaving. But the majority were arts traditional to Japan, such as *ikebana* (plant arranging), embroidery, and calligraphy. While some scholars have interpreted this through a more political and psychological lens (e.g., Dusselier 2008), others have associated it with the Japanese concept of *gaman*, which can be glossed as "enduring the seemingly unbearable with patience and dignity" (Hirasuna 2005, 1).

As Eaton (1952, 46) pointed out in his study, the art of each camp was shaped by both available natural resources and the skills of those within it. An inescapable element of the Amache landscape was the sand, which was both underfoot and in the air. Kunsen Ninomiya transformed this bane of camp life into the raw material of art. As she described it to Eaton, she and her two boys arrived at Amache during a sandstorm (16). Struggling through the experience, she recalled her training in the making of *bon-kei*, miniature landscapes in which sand could be "something else than dust and dirt" (16). The tray for her first arrangement was crafted by a neighbor from a packing crate, and she soon involved other neighbors, teaching them how to make similar pieces. *Bon-kei* proved so popular that Ninomiya began teaching much larger groups. An exhibition of the work of her nearly 100 pupils took place in November 1943; it was later extolled by Eaton as "the most extensive display of *bon-kei* ever seen in the western world" (16). A *Granada Pioneer* (1943b) article noted that the exhibit was visited by 3,000 people despite its location in one of the 100 foot × 20 foot Rec Hall buildings turned into the camp's Hospitality House.

A striking example of *gaman*, the making of *bon-kei* at Amache has often been highlighted by scholars (e.g., Limerick 1992). Other arts that were very common at Amache were painting and making artificial flowers out of a range of materials, especially paper. Woodcarving was another popular art form, and Eaton (1952, 12) suggests that incarcerees from Amache produced the greatest number of traditional Japanese-style wood carvings of the ten camps. In addition to its popularity, woodcarving shares another resemblance with *bon-kei* in that beyond the teachers, it was a new art form to most practitioners. Many families with Amache ties cherish the carvings made by their relatives in camp (figure 4.8), an art form few continued to practice afterward.

Echoing art practices, other activities in camp were often quintessentially American, like baseball and basketball games and, later, picnics along the nearby Arkansas River. Others had deep roots in Japan, like judo, sumo, traditional theater productions, and the celebration of Obon, a Buddhist festival that drew thousands of incarcerees each year (Harvey 2003). Some, like the frequent performances of hula in camp, reflected the experiences of Nikkei across the Japanese diaspora.

Work was an important part of life in camp, especially for those whose financial assets had been lost or seized. Incarcerees found employment on

FIGURE 4.8. Frances Palmer, with Toshiko (Sakamoto) Aiboshi, holds a wood carving made at Amache by her grandfather Shigeto Yoshimune. Author photograph taken at the 2009 Amache reunion.

the farms and ranches of Amache's agricultural program and within the camp at the many jobs required to keep it functioning, like the dozen or so workers employed in each mess hall. Wages, however, were remarkably low, set below the lowest rate for enlisted men in the United States Army (twenty-one dollars a month). Even the pharmacists, doctors, and dentists who worked in the camp hospital made only nineteen dollars a month.

The Granada Relocation Project administrator for the WRA was James G. Lindley. Another notable staff member was Joseph McClelland, the reports officer who was also the camp photographer and oversaw the newspaper, the *Granada Pioneer*. Lindley and his administration are regarded in a generally favorable light. Historian Robert Harvey (2003, 207) noted that the incarcerees who knew Lindley "felt he was an able administrator with a deep regard for fairness." A number of the teachers at Amache petitioned successfully to move to camp, in part to be able to better serve their students (Kjeldgaard 1998). Among the unposed photographs in Joseph McClelland's personal collection, are images of WRA staff and incarcerees playing cards together (figure 4.9). A WRA community analyst reported in early 1943 that relations between groups at Amache were "infinitely better" than those at any of the other WRA facilities and that the project administration functioned smoothly (Embree 1943). As Minoru Tonai noted, the credit for the quality of those relations "goes to Mr. Lindley and his staff, as well as [to] the school teachers, who cared" (personal communication 2018).

The WRA camps were much more porous than most imagine. Even at the assembly centers, inmates were able to apply for permits to work outside. With most young men away serving in the military, farmers faced an acute labor shortage at a time when production needs were rising. Surrounded by farms and ranches, many Amacheans found ready temporary or permanent employment as agricultural laborers in the vicinity. In 1943 alone, 1,428 Amacheans (well over 10% of the population) left the site on seasonal work leave (Heimburger 2008, 17). The generally positive relationship with regional farmers was fostered in part by the efforts of Amacheans in the fall of 1942. As the result of a combination of the wartime labor shortage and weather, the Colorado sugar beet harvest was under threat. Incarcerees came out of the camps, some as paid laborers but nearly 150 as volunteers, to help surrounding farmers bring in the crop (WRA 1945). Letters published in the *Granada Pioneer* document regional gratitude for this gracious act.

Young people in particular sought jobs outside camp because of the freedom from the restrictive environment and the significantly higher wages available (Heimburger 2013). Others who left soon were college students aided in particular by Quaker organizations committed to place them in willing institutions. As the military opened up service to those of Japanese ancestry (first as volunteers and then through induction), even more young adults left the camp. Indeed, as one community history notes, in time only those under eighteen and the elderly were left (Noda 1981).

Amache had the highest rate of military involvement of all the camps. A total of 953 men and women from Amache volunteered or were drafted for military service during World War II. Of that number, 105 were wounded and 31 were killed in action. Among those killed was Kiyoshi Muranaga, who was awarded the Congressional Medal of Honor. However, not all Amacheans responded favorably to the notice for induction into the military. Thirty-one men from Amache were tried for draft evasion, found guilty, and sent to prison in Tucson, Arizona. These conscientious objectors were

FIGURE 4.9. Personal photograph by camp photographer Joseph McClelland of incarcerees and staff playing cards at Amache. *Courtesy*, Amache Preservation Society, McClelland Collection, Granada, CO.

largely driven by a sense of injustice and refused to serve while their families were incarcerated.

Although many of the WRA camps had war-related industries, Amache was the only camp with a successful silkscreen shop. At the time, silkscreening was one of the best ways to crisply print in color, something required by the United States Navy for its training materials. Established in June 1943, the Amache silkscreen shop employed 45 people and produced over 250,000 color posters under a contract with the navy. The staff also created many prints for use in camp, including calendars, event programs, and souvenirs for the yearly carnival. The body of work produced by the Amache silkscreen shop comprises a visually distinctive record of life at the camp (figure 4.10).

The WRA agricultural program at Amache was also very successful. In 1943 alone, inmate farmers produced approximately 4 million pounds of vegetables, over 50,000 bushels of field crops, and eggs and milk for the camp, as well as successfully raising a wide range of livestock. As the editor of the *Granada Pioneer* extolled at the end of that year, "We must pay tribute to the farm workers who toiled in the cold weather and sweated in the sweltering heat so there would not be 6,000 or more empty stomachs during this

FIGURE 4.10. View of Amache landscape created by the artists at the Amache silk-screen shop. *Courtesy,* Amache Preservation Society, Granada, CO.

coming winter months" (Sako 1943a). Not only did the farmers of Amache make the camp self-sufficient for many foodstuffs, they often produced a surplus. For example, in the fall of 1943, Amache sent 600 bushels of spinach each to Poston and Gila (other WRA camps), with another 1,000 bushels sent to the United States Army (*Granada Pioneer* 1943c).

Amache's proximity to the town of Granada created a situation unique among the WRA camps. Incarcerees were close enough to Granada that walking into town to shop or visit a soda fountain was a common occurrence. Passes were generally granted for these activities, and the positive effect this had on camp morale was noted by the WRA (Embree 1943). Although some local businesses were anti-Japanese, most came to value Amachean customers. Indeed, the 1945 Amache High School annual was filled with advertising from businesses in Granada and Lamar. Newman Drug Company is a good example of a business connected to Amache. Before the opening of the camp,

Edward Newman rented one of the largest buildings in Granada and brought in stock he thought would appeal to the inmates, including an entire warehouse of saké (Harvey 2003). The Newman family employed Amacheans in the store and also as the family nanny (Bruce Newman, personal communication 2011), a practice fairly common in the area.

It wasn't just Caucasian-run businesses that catered to incarcerees. After gaining a release from Amache, Frank Tsuchiya started his own successful local business, the Granada Fish Market. Using his connections from running a fish market in Los Angeles, he was able to bring in *sashimi*-grade fish to Granada (Hosokawa 2005, 103). The store also sold Japanese food and condiments such as soy sauce and noodles, both hard to come by in the camp (Harvey 2003, 127). To increase access to their wares, many stores or individual proprietors came to Amache, including the Granada Fish Market, which made deliveries of fresh fish and chickens every other day (Chang 1997, 287). Evidence of these connections between camp and town are visible in the physical remains found during archaeological studies of Amache, including abalone shell that likely derives from the Granada Fish Market and swizzle sticks from a bar in Granada.

Freedom, Power, and Surveillance at Amache

Issues of power and freedom are key to understanding life at Amache or any site of institutional confinement (Casella 2007; Dowling 2014). Although modeled on military facilities, the WRA camps were also influenced by prison design, and the guard towers in particular facilitated and communicated visual surveillance. Lack of privacy also created a sort of internal surveillance, and incarcerees knew far more about their neighbors than they likely cared to (Dowling 2014). Some of the Amache survivors recall surveillance vividly; Lily Havey's (2014) camp memories are haunted by being followed at night by the light from the guard tower. Not all surveillance was so overt, however. The WRA hired sociological and anthropological researchers to study camp life, but they were also tasked with letting administrators know if foment was building in the community (Hirabayashi 1999). Some incarcerees themselves were involved in keeping tabs on their fellow residents, including the internal police force who were (with the exception of the chief) all Amacheans. Some people were considered *inu*, informers or spies, and in camps where tensions with administrators ran high, these people were under threat of violence from others in the community (Hayashi 2013). As reflected in WRA reports cited earlier, Amache seems to have been one of the camps with the least such friction; however, Yamato Ichihashi's writings illuminate factions in Amache and the ways administrators would sometimes intervene (Chang 1997).

Clearly, freedom of movement at Amache was circumscribed. There was a front gate at which visitors and incarcerees needed to report when coming and going. On a daily basis, people required a pass or a job outside of the camp boundaries to leave. After screening and assurances by sponsors, more permanent leaves were granted to people who had outside employment or were attending postsecondary educational institutions. As the war wore on, the borders of the camp became much less securely guarded. Indeed, many young Amacheans (especially the boys) remember ducking under the fence to hunt arrowheads or take the short cut into Granada.

Many anthropological discussions of locales of inequality are inspired by historical and sociological studies of power. Even in situations when one does not have administrative power (power over), one rarely lacks complete individual power (power to) (McGuire and Paynter 1991). This was certainly the case at Amache. For instance, many activities associated with pre-war Japanese American communities were banned in all the camps, including the drinking of alcohol and (at least in the beginning) owning or operating a camera. People and packages coming into Amache were supposed to be checked for such contraband, but as is clear from both oral histories and the archaeological record (Driver 2015; Slaughter 2006), alcohol in particular was both smuggled into and brewed within the camp. Another widely ignored regulation was the prescription against cooking in the barracks (Shew 2010).

How these power issues played out with regard to the camp landscape will be elucidated in the following chapters, but it does appear that incarcerees at Amache had fairly free rein when it came to the modification of their spaces. Indeed, the administration encouraged the construction of gardens in some instances, for example, by providing access to vehicles or allowing excursions out of camp to gather garden resources. It does appear that there was some friction around the use of water, as evidenced by oral histories and archival records. Just how much freedom Amacheans had when it came to changing their carcereal environment will likely never be known, but we can turn to the gardens themselves for some answers.

Agriculturalists at Amache

To better understand the professional backgrounds of those at Amache, I turned to the final accountability roster prepared by the War Relocation Authority. Although a troubling reflection of government surveillance (Geis and Soloman 2019), the roster contains significant information on each incarceree, including the area in which they lived prior to the war, their birthplace and that of their parents, and occupational information for those old enough to have engaged in paid employment. This last piece of data helps us understand the kinds of expertise people had before the war. By integrating this information with the camp directories, we can map how people with these different skills were distributed across the landscape.

To code interview data, the WRA compiled a long list of occupations with detailed definitions. Table 4.1 lists all those that relate to agriculture and horticulture and is inspired by a similar analysis of the population of Manzanar (Burton 2015, 81–91). I have included livestock growers as agriculturalists because, as in the case of the Fujita family discussed in chapter 3, most farmers who raise livestock also raise fodder. At Amache, 1,516 of the 3,662 people with an occupation listed were involved in agriculture or horticulture. They make up 41 percent of the population of formerly employed, but if we add in the people whose secondary or tertiary occupations were in those fields, the total rises to 1,764 people, or 48 percent of that population. Of individuals whose primary occupation is agriculture or horticulture, 702 were married men while only 183 were married women. Thus one suspects that many women involved in family businesses such as farms or nurseries are not included in those counts. I feel confident in saying that at least half, if not more, of adult Amacheans made their living before the war growing things.

Looking at the WRA data also helps us understand these professionals' backgrounds. Two-thirds (66%) of those involved in agriculture and horticulture were first-generation immigrants. Likewise, nearly the same ratio of those immigrants (57%) came from farming backgrounds in Japan and would have arrived in the United States with knowledge of the agricultural

TABLE 4.1. Agricultural and horticultural job titles recorded by the War Relocation Authority

Code	Title	Class*
349	Agricultural Occupations, N.E.C. [not elsewhere classified]	Agricultural
43160	Agricultural, Horticultural, and Kindred Occupations	Agricultural
36586	Agricultural, Horticultural, and Kindred Occupations	Agricultural
43162	Agricultural, Horticultural, and Kindred Occupations	Agricultural
43163	Agricultural, Horticultural, and Kindred Occupations	Agricultural
43161	Agricultural, Horticultural, and Kindred Occupations	Agricultural
307	Animal and Livestock Farmers	Agricultural
301	Cash Grain Farmers	Agricultural
302	Cotton Farmers	Agricultural
12	County Agents and Farm Demonstrators	Agricultural
303	Crop Specialty Farmers	Agricultural
304	Dairy Farmers	Agricultural
336	Farm Couples	Agricultural
317	Farm Hands, Animal and Livestock	Agricultural
312	Farm Hands, Cotton	Agricultural
313	Farm Hands, Crop Specialty	Agricultural
314	Farm Hands, Dairy	Agricultural
315	Farm Hands, Fruit	Agricultural
316	Farm Hands, General Farms	Agricultural
311	Farm Hands, Grain	Agricultural
318	Farm Hands, Poultry	Agricultural
319	Farm Hands, Vegetable	Agricultural
337	Farm Managers and Foremen	Agricultural
335	Farm Mechanics	Agricultural
3X1	Farming	Agricultural
330	Fruit and Vegetable Graders and Packers	Agricultural
305	Fruit Farmers	Agricultural
306	General Farmers	Agricultural
308	Poultry Farmers	Agricultural
348	Technical Agricultural Occupations, N.E.C.	Agricultural
309	Truck Farmers	Agricultural
201	Day Workers	Gardening
340	Gardeners and Grounds Keepers, Parks, Cemetaries [sic], Etc.	Gardening
204	Housemen and Yardmen	Gardening
339	Nursery and Landscaping Laborers	Nursery
338	Nursery Operators and Flower Growers	Nursery

* These classifications are inspired by Burton 2015, but I have separated out nursery workers into their own class.

practices of their homeland. When we look at just those who were in the gardening professions, the connections to Japan are even greater: 73 percent of them were Japanese immigrants. Nine of these gardeners came from urban prefectures where they were likely to have encountered formally designed gardens such as those discussed in chapter 3. Those gardeners born in the United States were primarily from California (23%), while 4 percent came from other states. Among the American-born gardeners, seven were Kibei, the majority having spent five or more years going to school in Japan. During their time in Japan, it is likely that they were exposed to formal Japanese gardening traditions.

Camp addresses are also available for the majority of these professionals. When we chart where individuals of the different agricultural professions were living at Amache, distinct clustering is evident (figure 4.11). This patterning likely represents regional occupational specialization and perhaps also the choice to live near those with whom an individual had a connection fostered through work. The regional source of professional clustering is particularly true of those from the Yamato farming colonies, with some blocks identified among former incarcerees with the hometown of their majority residents (for example, Block 10E is known as the "Cortez Block"). Five Amache blocks contained over seventy residents with an agricultural or horticultural background, while four others contained twenty or fewer such professionals. Significant clustering of those just from the gardening occupations is also evident, with five blocks containing fifteen or more gardeners. Still, at least one gardener lived in each of the occupied barracks blocks. Many blocks did not contain a single person from the nursery fields, while three of them housed five or more. How these occupational patterns played out in what we see regarding the quantity and character of landscaping and gardening at Amache is part of the story that unfolds in the chapters to follow.

Closing the Camp

A combination of legal and military battles drew the internment era to a close. As military success in the Pacific reduced concerns of a West Coast attack, the US Supreme Court weighed cases fighting the legality of the continued incarceration. Although earlier cases had been decided in favor of some aspects of the restriction of the rights of Japanese Americans, Mitsuye

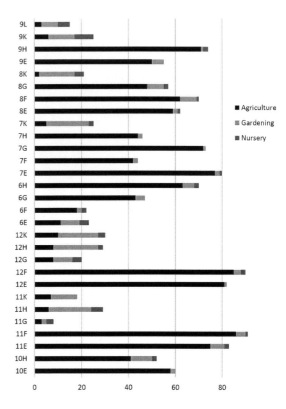

FIGURE 4.11. Graph of agricultural and horticultural professionals occupying each block at Amache. Block location compiled from the 1943 and 1945 camp directories.

Endo's case seemed likely to prevail. A US citizen, Endo had sworn her allegiance to her country (like most others in the camps) and yet continued to be incarcerated. Warned of the Court's decision, the new director of the army's Western Defense Command publicly announced on December 17, 1944, that exclusion of loyal Japanese American civilians from the West Coast would be terminated effective January 1945 (Daniels 1972). The next day the Supreme Court announced that it had ruled that the federal government could no longer detain any US citizen who was, like Endo "concededly loyal" (*Ex parte Mitsuye Endo*, 323 U.S. 283 [1944]).

Although a few individuals left immediately for their properties on the West Coast, they knew they were likely to face continued hostility. Many families left in the summer of 1945, by which time the surrender of Germany made the end of the war appear imminent and the camp's children had completed their school year. Yet in July there were still over 4,000 people at Amache, a sign of how few resources many incarcerees had outside of camp. Not only were they economically destitute, they had no place to which they could return.

Japan's surrender in mid-August marked the end of the war and pushed the time line for closure of all WRA facilities. In the fall of 1945, Amache incarcerees built a small structure at the camp cemetery out of the brick that once served as their barracks floors. Inside they erected a large stone memorial, as well as wooden planks bearing the names in Japanese of all 114 inmates who died in camp and the 31 soldiers from Amache who were killed in action. Amache officially closed on October 15, 1945.

Some lucky families were able to return to their homes and farms in California, especially those from the Yamato farming colonies. Others with little to return to stayed in the Arkansas River Valley or moved to Denver, taking advantage of new connections to Colorado made during the war. Chicago had been a key location for resettlement efforts at Amache, and many former incarcerees and their families continue to live in the Midwest. Everyone did their best to start their lives over, often avoiding talking about their wartime experience.

Following the closure of Amache, all but two buildings—the monument at the cemetery and a concrete structure built by the Amache Cooperative— were dismantled and removed from the site. Many of the buildings were destroyed, but a fair number were sold to area farms and schools (Colorado Preservation, Inc. 2010). The camp area was purchased by the Town of Granada, which continues to own the land and use the deep wells drilled for the WRA camp as the city water supply. For many years the town leased grazing rights on the property to local ranchers, but beyond the construction of a few water tanks, the central camp area remained largely undeveloped. Important exceptions are a housing development where the hospital once stood and a horse arena where the motor pool had once parked its vehicles. Thus many of the widespread changes to the landscape made by those who spent the war years at Amache remain, a physical testament to their time in this prison on the prairie.

5

Transforming the Landscape

In learning to read the landscape of the High Plains, a particularly important tip is to pay attention to trees. What species are they, and what is their setting? In the vicinity of Amache, the only naturally occurring trees are cottonwoods and willows growing near water.[1] Teaching my crews to pay attention to the trees at Amache has paid off; they have yet to discover a barrack block without them. Each one of those trees was either planted by an incarceree or grew from the roots of a tree that was.

Although Amache is located in Colorado, for many who associate the state with mountains and plateaus, the area feels much more like Kansas, which lies only 16 miles to the east. The site sits near the center of the High Plains, a geographic region located between the Rocky Mountains and the Great Plains. Sloping gently away from the mountains, the area is forever affected by them. Its soils are mostly washed down from the mountains by rivers flowing east.

---

1 Only three native species of trees can be found growing in the Arkansas River Valley of Prowers County, Colorado: the Peachleaf Willow (*Salix amygdaloides*) and the Eastern and the Plains Cottonwood, which are both subspecies of *Populus deltoides*.

DOI: 10.5876/9781646420933.c005

The High Plains climate similarly owes its character to the mountains; they create a rain shadow and increase wind convection. The result is a dry and windy prairie, with native vegetation that can thrive in such a setting—low grasses, brush, and cacti, with moisture-loving species like cattails and choke-cherries growing along waterways or near springs (Clark and Scheiber 2008).

Although the soils immediately adjacent to the Arkansas River are suitable for agriculture, the central portion of the camp was located on a terrace above those lands and to the south of the river. Basically, the entire site sits on an only moderately stabilized sand dune created over the course of millennia by winds that pick up the sands from the riverbed and redeposit them to the south (Sharps 1976). Just how fragile the regional soils are was all too evident to those in the region who lived through the Dust Bowl years. In the areas of the camp where erosion or excavation reveals deep soil deposits, one can see sediments from the Dust Bowl era. The region was barely recovering from that erosional nightmare when construction of Amache started the whole process again. Bulldozing the central square mile of the camp removed the native vegetation that was just regaining a hold. Such an impact would not have been as devastating if the region weren't so arid and windy and the soil on which the site was built so sandy.

The shortgrasses prairie on which Amache sits has a certain majesty, especially in the spring when native wildflowers carpet the ground under big open skies. But for incarcerees coming from the towns and farms of California, the setting was another assault. Both period documents and recollections of former incarcerees document the significant dismay people felt when first encountering the denuded camp landscape. As one former incarceree recalled, her first thoughts were "oh my god, we are going to live here? It was so stark and desolate" (cited in Harvey 2003, 77). Another reported to the administration, "The slightest indication of wind to us in this center is a depressing thought. Because with it comes the inevitable sand and dust storms. The thoroughness with which it strains our nerves and adds to our restlessness, aside from the damage it does to our worldly belongings[,] cannot be over-estimated" (cited in WRA 1943b, 3). One of the strongest memories Carlene Tanigoshi Tinker, one of our former incarceree volunteers, has of her time at Amache was of being carried on her father's shoulders through a sandstorm. She recalls that he wrapped her head and face in a scarf to protect her from the blowing sand (personal communication 2010). Those memories have strongly stayed with Amacheans, impacting them to this day. As May Murakami told me, "Every time the wind blows, I always think of camp" (personal communication 2015).

But those who were—unwillingly—to make this their home did not merely accept these conditions. They set about almost immediately to transform the raw military facility into something more habitable. Trees and other landscaping can be found not just in the barracks block but in public blocks too, such as the one that housed the elementary school and the camp cooperative. There is variability, however, in both the history of how the trees came to Amache and in how they were planted. In some blocks, the trees were purchased from a nursery, but in others the trees were native cottonwoods, dug up from along the Arkansas River and transplanted at Amache (DU Amache 2009). Where some blocks have only a few trees in public areas, others clearly had a block-wide landscaping scheme with trees placed consistently throughout. Several facing blocks feature an avenue of trees along the road that separates them (figure 5.1), while other blocks that back up to each other share a park-like space along an otherwise invisible boundary. Many tree arrangements were clearly part of more elaborate landscaping, and we find them today often encircled with hardscaping, especially limestone but also river cobble, gravel, and other materials. One of the stills from the Amache home movies provides a good example (figure 5.2).

Because planting trees was perhaps the single-most-impactful modification to the camp landscape, my exploration of Amache's gardens and gardeners begins with two very different groups who nonetheless were critical to creating the site's treescape: people associated with nurseries and children. The former brought their expertise to bear at Amache, while the latter drew on their own experience outside of camp to insist on a livable landscape within it. Because of the importance of family businesses, some Amacheans were both; they were young people with experience in nurseries.

Nursery Families and Trees

Among the many satisfactions of working at a site of living memory have been ongoing conversations with those who have a personal tie to the camp. Years before archaeology crews put shovel to earth at Amache, I began a fruitful correspondence with Thomas Shigekuni. Although a lawyer by trade,

FIGURE 5.1. 2019 Aerial photograph showing trees lining the road between Blocks 11H and 11K, with 11H at the top. *Courtesy,* Jim Casey and Sensefly.

FIGURE 5.2. Public garden at Amache with limestone alignment and rock rings around trees. This still was captured from a 16 mm movie made at Amache. *Courtesy,* Amache Preservation Society, Tsukuda Collection, Granada, CO.

Mr. Shigekuni has a love of history. When the Amache Historical Society first started its reunions, he gathered and reproduced important historical documents to share with his fellow former incarcerees. Among those documents were reports about agriculture in camp. Mr. Shigekuni has a strong personal interest in these issues, in part because of his family background. Before the war, his family was in the nursery business. They were among the fifty-six people noted on the accountability roster who were similarly employed prior to the war.

Tom's father, Yonetaro, was a gardener, and he saved cuttings from plants for propagation. Shizuyo Shigekuni, Tom's mother, started the business with those cuttings, growing plants on 2 acres of land next to the family home in Los Angeles (Vicki Wong, email correspondence 2015). Shizuyo transplanted the cuttings into 1- and 3-gallon cans that Tom, then a young boy, would water (Shigekuni 2011). The business did well, and eventually the Shigekunis opened Inglewood Park Nursery on La Brea. It was a family business, but legally the owner was the oldest Shigekuni son, Tsuneo, an American citizen (US Selective Service System 1942). Tsuneo, who was twenty-six when the war broke out, left Amache in April 1943 to work in Milwaukee (WRA 1946). Tom was only twelve or so when they were sent to the camp, but his older brother Henry (who appears as Masaaki in the WRA records) was about seventeen and was thus experienced as a nursery worker.

Tom recalled, in both an oral history and a written letter, the important role his family played in planting trees at the camp (Shigekuni 2011). The Shigekuni family was housed, along with a number of others from Los Angeles, in Block 12G, which was at the far south end of camp. Tom recalled that his brother Henry traveled the 17 miles to Lamar to get trees for the residents of the block. Henry chose a variety that both currently and historically are often referred to as Chinese elm, but are in fact Siberian elm (*Ulmus pumila*). As Tom recalled, Henry knew that the trees would go dormant in the winter and thus be a good fit for Colorado. He chose wisely, as today only the Siberian elms have survived at Amache. The trees were of moderate size, about 6 feet tall, and they cost 50 cents each. Because Henry knew something about successful transplantation, he insisted that the nursery provide bales of peat moss with which to plant the trees. Although he procured the trees for the entire block, it was up to individuals or families to plant the trees in front of their barracks. In the Shigekuni family (and likely others) it was the job of the teenage sons to plant and, later, water their trees. Tom's father, Yonetaro, did not seem to be involved in planting the 12G trees, despite expertise derived from his time as a gardener and nurseryman. It is likely that Yonetaro's employment as a janitor and cook for the mess hall kept him too busy. His main job, with which Tom sometimes helped, was to make the rice eaten by the hundreds of occupants of 12G, a task that involved washing and cooking 100 pounds of rice each day (Shigekuni 2011).

FIGURE 5.3. 2019 aerial photograph showing trees in Block 12G. *Courtesy*, Jim Casey and Sensefly.

Mr. Shigekuni's recollections, in combination with the data derived from survey, provide valuable insight into landscaping practices at Amache. As revealed through survey and aerial photographs, Block 12G had fairly consistent landscaping (figure 5.3), despite the fact that it is one of the blocks where fewer than twenty individuals were professionally involved in agriculture or horticulture. Trees in 12G were primarily planted along public buildings and in locations where barrack entryways faced each other. This practice was a strong contributing factor to the feeling that the entry side of barracks (where the doors were located) was the front yard and that backyards existed behind the buildings. In some blocks the placement of trees was notably regular, for example, in Block 7H, where they were placed almost exactly 6 feet from the doorways and were part of integrated, barrack-long gardens (figure 5.4a, 5.4b). Block 7H had an average number of agriculture and horticulture professionals (42), but unlike 12G, none of them were in the nursery business. Still, in 7H it appears that the planting of trees was a communal endeavor; otherwise the landscape would be less cohesive. In 12G, tree placement was not as regimented, which likely reflects what we know from oral history: that individuals planted their own trees. Still, there were also communal efforts at improvement in the Shigekunis' block, as indicated by the rows of trees planted in public areas, like the alignment of trees along the mess hall.

The Shigekunis were among the families of nursery operators who helped shape Amache. As explored in the research of Erin Riggs (2013), a field school

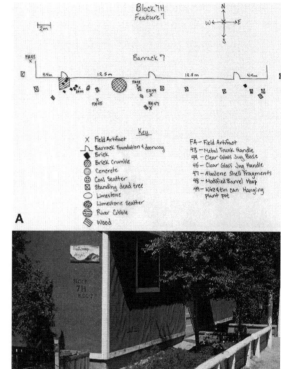

FIGURE 5.4A. Map of
Block 7H, Barrack 7
entryway gardens as they
appeared to archaeology
crews in 2016. *Courtesy,*
DU Amache Project,
inked by Emerson Klever.

FIGURE 5.4B. Historical
photograph of south-
west corner of the same
entryway gardens taken
by camp photographer
Joseph McClelland.
Courtesy, Amache
Preservation Society,
Granada, CO.

student in the summer of 2012, the Domoto family also strongly influenced
the landscape of the camp. The patriarch of the family was Kanetaro Domoto,
an Issei who in 1892 used his savings as a fruit peddler to purchase land in
Oakland, California (*Granada Pioneer* 1943d). By 1908, Domoto Brothers was
"the largest importer of nursery stock on the Pacific Coast" (Payne 1909, 3627).
The nursery eventually encompassed over 40 acres of Bay-area land, with
housing for the family and workers. Unfortunately, the Domoto Brothers'
nursery did not survive the Great Depression (Riggs 2013); however, two of
Kanetaro's sons would continue his legacy. The oldest, Toichi, who began his
training as an engineer, established his own successful nursery in Hayward,
California, eventually patenting several new species of plants (Riggs 2013).

A younger son, Kaneji, turned to landscape architecture, taking classes at Stanford and the University of California, Berkeley.

Kaneji Domoto's initial training in Japanese landscape design came when he, along with other area Nisei, were hired as laborers to assist master Japanese gardeners. The gardeners were in the Bay area on the behest of the Japanese government to create a garden on Treasure Island for the 1939 International Exposition (see figure 3.4 for a photograph of that garden). Because of Kaneji's contribution to that garden, he was subsequently hired to assist with the Japanese garden at the 1940 New York International Exposition (Riggs 2013). While in New York, Kaneji wrote to Frank Lloyd Wright, requesting a position as an apprentice. He was accepted and drove directly from New York to join Wright at Taliesen, in Spring Green, Wisconsin (Riggs 2013). While an apprentice at Taliesen, Kaneji came to appreciate the way Wright, who had done notable work in Japan, translated many Japanese design elements into his own organic modernism (Riggs 2013). Within the year, Kaneji was back in the Bay area of California, designing a garden in nearby Gilroy (Kris Marubayashi, personal communication 2019).

As noted in chapter 3, two different exclusion zones were created along the West Coast. The Domotos were among the families who moved out of Military Area no. 1 in the hopes of avoiding forced removal. Toichi, in the face of Kanetaro's age and failing health, had taken over leadership of the family. He moved his father and immediate family to his sister's home in Livingston, California (Riggs 2013), and they were joined there by Kaneji and his family (Kris Marubayashi, personal communication 2019). Unfortunately, the strategy failed, for in California both Areas no. 1 and 2 were eventually "evacuated." Rather than living with friends from the Bay area, the Domotos were incarcerated at Amache along with families from the Central Valley of California.

Camp records help us follow the Domotos once they arrived at Amache. It appears that at first, three generations of family members—Kanetaro and his daughters, Wakako and Yuriko; Toichi, his wife, Alice, and their two young children; and Kaneji, his wife, Sally, and their newborn—were all housed in a single 20 foot × 24 foot barrack room in Block 6H. The camp directory information is somewhat contradictory, but it appears that in early 1943 the family was able to move into at least two separate units, with Kanetaro and Kaneji's family moving to Block 6F while Toichi's immediate family and his sisters moved to Block 6G. In the spring of 1943, Kaneji was elected block representative for 6F (*Granada Pioneer* 1943e). Sadly, Kanetaro was among the over 100 incarcerees who did not survive Amache. He passed away in 1943, and his ashes are buried in the family plot in Oakland.

Toichi served on the Amache school board and appears to have spent much of his time managing the family and his nursery back home, which fortunately was in the hands of a trusted employee (Riggs 2013). Kaneji, in contrast, took up employment as an architectural draftsman in the camp's engineering division. The *Granada Pioneer* occasionally ran spotlight pieces on members of the Amache community, including one on Kaneji on May 15, 1943. It discusses how he designed the landscaping for the public areas of Block 6F. Perhaps overstating the case, the article claimed that through his efforts in that block, Kaneji was the "fellow that started the ball rolling in the center's beautification program" (Sako 1943b, 5). Certainly, he does appear to have been active in a number of such efforts. Only a few weeks earlier the *Pioneer* published his plans for a porch and landscaping at the entryway of the camp's Boy Scout Headquarters (figure 5.5). Our survey in the block where the headquarters building was located confirms that his plans came to fruition.

It is illustrative to look at the design Kaneji employed for the Block 6F landscaping. Rather than the rectilinear arrangements so common in other blocks, the trees in the public spaces of 6F are in more natural groupings (figure 5.6). It seems likely that Kaneji's design choices were influenced by his experience with Japanese design, which, particularly in gardens, tends toward asymmetrical arrangements meant to evoke natural groupings. This is a design ideal Kaneji and his coauthor George Kay later promoted in *Bonsai and the Japanese Garden: Applying the Ancient Bonsai Art and Japanese Landscaping to America's Gardens* (1974). The book specifically urges garden designers to mimic arrangements found in nature (Domoto and Kay 1974, 41, 51). Although much of his landscape design at Amache is accessible only archaeologically, visitors to the Japanese garden at the Berkeley Botanical Gardens can see Kaneji's subtle craft at work. His legacy with Frank Lloyd Wright lives on in the examples of Usonian homes he designed in the late 1940s (Voon 2017).

The Shigekunis and the Domotos were among the hundreds, if not thousands, of incarcerees who invested their time and money in creating and maintaining Amache's treescape. Trees transformed the landscape and provided definitive environmental benefits. Tree roots helped stabilize the soil,

COURTESY OF KAN DOMOTO

FIGURE 5.5. Plans for Boy Scout Headquarters published in the *Granada Pioneer* (April 28, 1943). *Courtesy*, Japanese Americans in World War II Collection, Special Collections Research Center, California State University, Fresno.

an effect with which all the agriculture and horticulture professionals in the camp would have been familiar. Watering trees would have created, if only temporarily, more humid microclimates. Finally, trees provided shade in the summer in an otherwise often hot and sunny location. That role in particular seems to have impacted activities at Amache. Children's play often took place in the shade of trees, as evidenced by where we find marbles and other toys. For example, in Block 11H, we located ten marbles, most of them within a foot or two of a tree. Throughout the camp we have discovered tokens near trees, indicating they were popular locations for adult games like *go*.

In 2018, the archaeological work at Amache focused on a newly returned recreation hall in Block 11F. Planned work to protect and renovate the building will likely impact the ground around it, so crews investigated the area all around to make sure no important resources would be affected by that

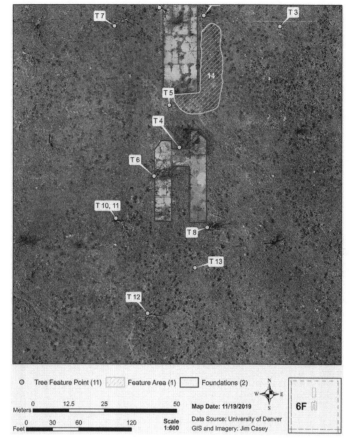

FIGURE 5.6. Map of central area of Block 6F indicating the locations of trees. *Courtesy*, Jim Casey.

work. A combination of surface survey and ground-penetrating radar (GPR) revealed that five trees had been planted at 5 meter to 6 meter intervals all along the south side of the recreation hall. We set up a series of excavation units to investigate what other landscaping might have been present in this area in addition to the trees. Excavations revealed few obvious signs of landscaping besides tantalizing clues that the area once featured an entry gate. Our investigations also uncovered lots and lots of marbles, some on the surface and some buried in the soft Amache sand. They indicate that the area saw significant use as a play space.

Sediments from the likely gate posthole and a few other locations in the excavations were tested for microscopic evidence of the plants that might have once grown in this space—both pollen and phytoliths. Those of us with seasonal allergies are all too familiar with the notion that flowering plants create pollen to reproduce, but phytoliths are a lesser-known phenomenon. The term *phytoliths* literally means plant stones in Latin, and they are small silica bodies that provide structural stability for a number of plant species. Like pollen, their shape and size yield clues as to the family of the plant that produced them. In the 11F samples, analyst John G. Jones (2019) recovered notably high grass pollen counts along with phytoliths from the *Festucoid* grass family. Favoring cool climates, these samples likely reflect ornamental grasses planted in this area along with the trees. Much of the other pollen recovered is of the type that is spread over great distances by the wind, but a few grains of more locally dispersed pollen from likely ornamental species were recovered, including those from the rose family (*Rosaceae*) and prairie clover (*Dalea*), an attractive native wildflower. Interestingly, the sediments included pollen representing the parsley family (*Apiaceae*) (Jones 2019). Although most plants in this family are vegetables (like carrots) or herbs (such as parsley and fennel), they do have attractive leaves and a pleasant scent. Japanese garden guides note that such spaces should appeal to all the senses, and plants from the parsley family would have helped this landscaped space do just that.

We also did ground-penetrating radar and opened up a single test unit on the north side of the 11F recreation hall. We found no evidence that trees were planted on that side of the building. This revelation is particularly interesting because the north side of the building faced a public use block that held the Amache ball fields. As such, landscaping on that side of the building would have been seen by far more of the camp's population. Yet the trees on the south side would have shaded the building, and that appears to have been the priority for the residents of Block 11F.

Important discoveries about the 11F landscape continued after the field school. Carlene Tanigoshi Tinker, who helped us with both the GPR and the excavations in 11F, returned to some documents related to her time as a little girl in camp. Much to her (and the crew's) delight, she realized that the 11F recreation hall was where she had attended pre-school. The tree line along the south side of the building would have helped temper the heat for the little tykes who spent part of their day inside and part of their day outside, at least a few of them playing marbles. The people of Block 11F definitely knew how to nurture those trees. It was one of the blocks where over seventy occupants were from the agricultural fields, although only one of them was associated with a nursery.

The treescape of Amache likely conferred other benefits to the incarcerees. The High Plains are a stark, open landscape, often unbroken for miles by anything other than short grasses, brush, and cactus. Trees break up that monotony, providing a soothing green counterpoint to what is in essence a desert. They likely were also physiologically, not just psychologically, beneficial. Multiple studies of populations under stress indicate that exposure to trees yields significant benefits. For example, surgery patients who can see trees from their hospital rooms heal faster (Ulrich 1984). Likewise, Japanese who participate in *shinrin-yoku*, mindfully walking through a forest (literally, forest bathing), report decreased hostility and depression and increased liveliness (Morita et al. 2007). Although as a modern practice *shinrin-yoku* would not have been familiar to Amacheans, the belief on which it is founded—the beneficial power of nature—was likely shared by most of them.

Growing in Camp: Students and the School Grounds

It was not just the adult population at Amache that contributed to remaking its landscape. In an article written during the war, educators in the Amache Elementary School documented how children transformed their school grounds (Dumas and Walther 1944). As the article notes, "Schools, housed in barrack rooms, were so arranged that passage from room to room, to library, office, or lavatory, could be attained only by stepping out in the periodic fury of dust and sand" (Dumas and Walther 1944, 40). Students in two sixth-grade art classes discussed solutions to their inhospitable setting. Likely influenced by the efforts of their parents and neighbors in other areas of the camp, the children suggested that the entire school block be landscaped. It was to be a design competition; after meeting as a committee with adult incarcerees, fifty children submitted landscaping plans for the school (Dumas and Walther 1944). As with all but the administrative, hospital, and cemetery areas, the school grounds were not irrigated; thus the children's plans needed to accommodate a largely xeriscapic environment.

One way to do so was to choose low-water varieties of grass, and the article notes that some designs incorporated rye grass. Another source for low-water plants was the local environment. It appears that transplanting natives was also a tactic chosen by the student garden designers. Articles in both the English- and Japanese-language portions of the *Granada Pioneer* (1944) recruited volunteers for a trip to the Arkansas River to dig up shrubs to be transplanted on the school grounds.

Archaeology is another avenue for understanding the elementary school grounds. April Kamp-Whittaker (2010) was interested in how children related to the landscape of the camp. So it was a natural fit for us to investigate the elementary school block in 2008. Intensive survey there suggested a similarity in the size and placement of the individual garden beds. It is also clear that the edges of these beds were delineated by limestone, although now this is revealed primarily through linear scatters of decaying stone. Limestone is the bedrock that underlays most of Amache. It was accessible in a few outcrops near camp and would also have been a by-product of the construction of subterranean camp facilities. Historical photographs of some of the landscaped areas capture regular, linear outlines of limestone (figure 5.7), confirming our survey data, which revealed a systematic landscaping scheme.

Students took their own initiative within these design parameters. To better investigate what their choices might have been, excavated units were placed in two different garden beds that flanked a doorway of one of the classroom barracks. The beds in this pair were approximately the same size and were both bounded by limestone outlines. However, excavation revealed that the children who designed them put into place quite different kinds of schemes. One of these beds was landscaped with consistently sized gravel that almost certainly came from the banks of the Arkansas River. The adjacent bed had no gravel. We recovered ornamental morning glory seeds (*Ipomoea*) from one bed but none from the other.

One of the photographs accompanying the historical journal article shows a young Caucasian woman and a line of little Japanese girls standing along the edge of a prepared bed. The caption reads, "The teacher shows one of the little girls how to scatter seeds" (Dumas and Walther 1944, 41). This caption implies that these children needed to be taught gardening skills, an assumption that counters the pre-camp experience many of them would have had with their family farms or related businesses. And indeed, the

FIGURE 5.7. Historical photograph of elementary school garden construction. Note the students working and the limestone boundaries of garden beds. Government document available on Calisphere.

excavated garden beds indicated that some of these children already knew a good deal about transforming the land and were applying that knowledge to the camp's arid setting in very different ways.

Archaeology highlights the paternalism of these historical documents, but, more important, it indicates ways children were important actors in transforming Amache. Not only was the landscaping their idea, the plans they created indicate individual preferences. Young children at Amache had nascent aesthetic senses of how the landscape should be. In this way, they were part of a long tradition that extended back to their ancestral homeland. A desire for landscaped grounds was also informed by the experience of many of these children in the American school system. Progressive-era ideas about the role of nature in education (Trelstad 1997) proscribed that schools should have landscaped grounds. Historical photographs of some of the schools attended by the children of Amache before the war (Uchima and Shinmoto 2010) suggest that children from Los Angeles attended elementary schools

FIGURE 5.8. Historical photograph of trees at Amache Elementary School immediately after planting. *Courtesy,* Amache Preservation Society, McClelland Collection, Granada, CO.

with landscaped grounds (e.g., 37th Street School), while many from the Central Valley did not (e.g., Vincent Grammar School in Merced County).

Publications for educators of the era included detailed prescriptions for how grounds should be designed: "There should be shade around the edge of school grounds. A double row of trees should be planted just outside the sidewalk and just inside the fence line" (Curtis 1927, 472). Photographs of the newly landscaped Amache Elementary School capture such a line of trees along the west edge of the block (figure 5.8). By insisting that their school was landscaped, the urban children of Amache were making their own environment much more familiar; a real school had grounds.

Survivors of Time

It takes imagination for visitors today to picture the camp as it was during occupation. There are three elements in particular that help with that vision: the intact road system, the hundreds of concrete building foundations, and the thousands of trees that dot the square-mile facility. Many of these trees, remarkably, are living survivors from World War II. Some are second or third generation, sprouted from roots of the parent trees. This is particularly the case for trees growing out of foundations; they are taking advantage of the water that often pools on the concrete after a rain. Other trees have succumbed to the years and either stand as skeletons or have fallen over. Each of these trees is a testament to a camp-wide effort to create a more livable environment. The trees continue their work to this day, providing shelter for the many birds that now make their home in this de facto wildlife refuge as well as shade for site visitors and archaeology crews.

As explored in this chapter, the expertise of some Amacheans helped them successfully and beautifully remake their unwilling home. Not everyone involved in the effort knew, like the Domoto and Shigekuni families did, specific techniques to transplant a tree. But the ability and the will to thrive in inhospitable settings were habits most Amacheans, including the children of the camp, did have. Before the war, many successfully farmed land others saw as unproductive. Businessmen saw promise in things that others threw away, like plant cuttings and old tin cans. That make-do and persistence is captured in oral histories, and the camp landscape remains a storehouse for evidence of how it took place at Amache.

6

Making Connections

Gardens are appealing, in part as respite from the outside world; they are a
place to get away. The gardens at Amache would have served that purpose
well, places of color and life contrasting vividly with drab barracks buildings.
But gardens also connect people, through the resources needed to make them,
the work of creating and caring for them, time spent together enjoying them,
and, in some cases, the plants they produce. This chapter explores the ways
gardens at Amache connected people and places at different spatial scales.
Within the camp they connected families, neighborhoods, and the entire community. They also helped people connect outside of camp, to the nation and
the Japanese diaspora. A close examination of how these gardens were made
and what they held reveals both expected and unexpected linkages.

Mothers and Gardens

When talk among former incarcerees turns to the food served in the mess halls,
it evokes memories that are vivid and largely unpleasant. As noted in chapter 4,

DOI: 10.5876/9781646420933.c006

Anita Miyamoto Miller was a very young girl during camp and has few memories of her incarceration. But she does remember hot dogs—lots and lots of hot dogs. In recalling those memories for her archaeology crewmates, Anita often screws up her face in disgust. She didn't eat another hot dog for decades after her camp experience. Although the inmate cooks worked hard and did the best they could, they often started out with ingredients that were at the lower end of the palatability scale. For example, one of the meat products provided to mess halls was beef tongue, which many Americans (whether of Japanese descent or not) consider a by-product. Its appearance on the camp menu is recalled with great distaste. Cottage cheese was also common early on in the camp (Skiles and Clark 2010), but it was an unfamiliar and potentially gastrically problematic food for people of Asian descent, who are often dairy intolerant.

One way for incarcerees to take at least some control of their cuisine was through gardening. Growing vegetables, berries, herbs, and fruit increased the palatability and nutritional content of their diets. Many Amacheans—individually, as families, or in groups—raised significant garden crops. Those who did so came from many backgrounds. Masae "Miki" Yasuhira was one of the two registered nurses at the Amache hospital. As highlighted in the *Granada Pioneer*, Yasuhira hailed from Fresno. Although the article focused mostly on her work as a nurse, it noted that she spent her free time at Amache in her vegetable garden (Sako, 1943c).

When it comes to connecting through food, however, our sights should turn to the camp mothers. Dana Ogo Shew's (2010) research shows that women in camp were reclaiming their traditional familial roles through cooking, despite regulations against preparing food in the barracks. Some of the most important foods mothers prepared came from their gardens.

One such garden was propagated by the Hiranos, who lived in Block 8F along with other incarcerees from Sonoma County. I have enjoyed discussing life in camp with George and Shig Hirano on a number of occasions. Mr. Hirano also introduced me to his mother, Kiyo's, published memoir, *Enemy Alien* (Hirano 1983). One interesting focus of her recollections about life in Amache was her work in one of the camp mess halls. But she also prepared food in her barracks. There were five boys in the Hirano family, and Kiyo made use of their labor to create a garden in front of their barrack (8F–12E). Photographs of Kiyo and her boys capture her growing family and garden over the time of the camp (figure 6.1). George remembers distinctly

FIGURE 6.1. The Hirano family in their Block 8F garden. *Courtesy*, George Hirano.

that his mother led them in laying out the family garden, and they dug "as she directed" (Hirano 2011). He recalls that the soil was very poor (something to which the soil chemistry also attests), so they dug it very deep. Although he does not remember amending the soil at that time, George suspects that it likely happened (Hirano 2014).

As captured in family photographs, the Hiranos gardened in a thin strip directly adjacent to their barrack and also in the center of what George referred to as the "street" between the two facing barracks (Hirano 2014). Calling it the "street" seems to reflect the layout in most other barracks blocks, where entryway gardens were only located adjacent to barracks. That plan left a broad open area in the center for foot (and occasionally car) traffic. Our intensive pedestrian survey in Block 8F suggests that a front yard arrangement of dual pathways with a garden in between was widespread throughout the block. Although this is the only barracks block we have surveyed where this pattern was common, it may be present in other blocks yet to be surveyed. Such median gardens would have been shared by neighbors whose doorways faced one another. George recalls that in laying out their garden, his mother made sure the boys were careful to use only the space that was theirs (2014).

FIGURE 6.2. Amache gardener carrying water retrieved from the barrel behind him. This still was captured from a 16 mm movie made at Amache. *Courtesy*, Amache Preservation Society, Tsukuda Collection, Granada, CO.

In the Hirano family (like the Shigekunis discussed in chapter 5), the teen-age boys' landscaping work did not end with digging; it was also their job to water plants. George recalled that he and his brothers carried water to the gardens with big cans scavenged from the mess hall and strung together with rope, a practice also captured in Amache home movies (figure 6.2). The Hirano boys used these buckets to carefully water each plant, which included cucumbers and squash. The cucumbers were destined to become Japanese pickles, which his mother made in a crock (Hirano 2011). Numerous stoneware crock fragments discovered in survey throughout the camp indicate that many gardeners likely grew vegetables specifically to be made into Japanese pickles. Unfortunately, large downed trees make it impossible for us to test the Hiranos' garden, but in 2008 and again in 2010 we investigated other vegetable gardens at Amache through test excavations. What we found in those gardens is featured at the end of this chapter.

Connecting a Neighborhood: Block Gardens

Main roads ran around a group of four barracks blocks, giving each block two more public, visible edges. In Block 11H, which was occupied primarily by incarcerees from Los Angeles, we discovered an intriguing garden that ran the length of one of its barracks. Unlike an entryway garden, it ran along the back of Barrack 1, where there were no doorways, and was placed immediately between the building and the road. It would have been very visible to all who passed by, a way to distinguish this block from its neighbors. Such a garden is fitting given that 11H was one of the blocks with twenty or more residents in the gardening professions, including five who were associated with nurseries.

This garden was first identified during survey in 2012; based on what could be seen on the surface, it appeared to employ two very different designs. The eastern portion of the garden was marked primarily by trees placed at regular 6 meter intervals. The western portion of the garden was marked by two standing and one fallen concrete pieces (figure 6.3). These "standing stones" are of varying heights, some with evidence of wood impressions and in one case a nail still embedded in the concrete. These garden decorations appear to be a by-product of how the building foundations were made at Amache. Wooden forms were placed directly onto the native soil, and then concrete was poured into them. The uneven ground surface and the haste with which the buildings were constructed often led to concrete oozing out of the bottom of the wooden forms. This created something like a horizontal concrete icicle, sometimes with only a thin piece connecting it to the foundation. Some likely broke off of their own accord, but if not, they could be removed with a little force. For people accustomed to gardens with standing stones, these long, narrow concrete pieces apparently looked like they would do the trick.

In 2016, we opened up a series of test excavations in the west side of the 11H Barrack 1 garden. What we found profoundly changed our view of this garden. In one of the test excavations, we recovered the clear evidence of a large planting hole surrounding a large decaying root. Together, they mark the location of a tree that once grew in this garden. It was found exactly 18 meters from the westernmost tree still standing in the garden and the same distance south from the barrack (figure 6.4). This find suggests that the systematic planting of trees at 6 meter intervals ran the entire length of the

FIGURE 6.3. Photograph of 11H, Barrack 1 garden with concrete "standing stones" circled. Author photograph, spring 2017.

garden. So rather than an American-style tree line on one side and a more Japanese-style stone garden on the west side, the two traditions were integrated. The trees and the concrete standing stones stood together throughout the garden. A similar mess hall garden was captured in Amache home movies (figure 6.5).

There also appear to have been additional plantings between the tree and stone alignments and the building in this garden. Excavation in a unit closer to the barrack foundation revealed another garden planting, likely either a small tree or a shrub. During excavation, it became clear that the roots of the original plant were surrounded by a 5 cm thick rind of grayish, silty clay, a soil type very different from the surrounding sand. A field trip to the

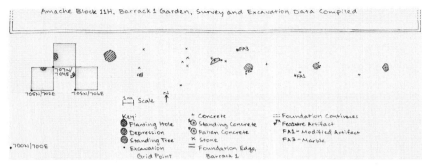

FIGURE 6.4. Map of Block 11H, Barrack 1 garden compiled from both survey and excavation data. *Courtesy*, DU Amache Project, map drawn by Courtney Seffense.

FIGURE 6.5. Mess hall garden as a meal starts at Amache. Note combination of trees and standing stones. This still was captured from a 16 mm movie made at Amache. *Courtesy*, Amache Preservation Society, Tsukuda Collection, Granada, CO.

Arkansas River indicates that the soil in that planting hole is similar to the soil along the banks of the river. But confirmation of its origin came in the lab. Although they were not conclusive as to the tree or shrub that was transplanted there, the pollen and phytoliths found in that rind are marked by species expected in a wetter, riverside setting, including Festucoid grasses (Jones 2017). Such grasses, including the attractive bulrush, are common in local wetlands (Roath et al. 2008, 291). Likewise, the chemistry of the rind's soil is rich in calcium and bicarbonate, both of which are elevated in the soils deposited by the Arkansas River (Seffense 2019).

As noted in chapter 5, many trees planted at Amache were purchased from nurseries. But former incarcerees also recall that some people dug up and transplanted trees and other plants they found along the Arkansas River. Atsushi Kikuchi recalled that "on the weekends people went outside to find some trees along the river. Volunteers got together, went out, dug trees, and planted them around the barracks" (cited in Gesensway and Roseman 1987, 48). Our previous four seasons of survey and excavation had not revealed discrete remains of this practice; however, in the 11H Barrack 1 excavations we seem to have uncovered robust evidence that the creators of this garden transplanted a tree or shrub along with its native soil to this location. In this garden we've also found intriguing evidence that is wasn't just plants gardeners were after at the Arkansas. The same elevated levels of calcium and bicarbonate were found in the larger excavated planting hole (Seffense 2019), the one that likely held a tree purchased from a nursery. It appears that the garden's builders were using soil from the Arkansas as amendment, and so its presence in any planting hole was not necessarily a by-product of transplantation but a deliberate choice. Not only would such soil retain moisture better because of its higher clay content, it was also much higher in organic material.

Wise use of natural resources and found objects are two aspects of Japanese gardening tradition that this garden employs well. This garden also helps us explore an important cultural legacy that is a little less obvious: units of measurement. Although Japan formally adopted the metric system during the Meiji era as part of its modernization program, those units of measurement were not part of public education until the 1920s (Hashimoto 1998). Craftsmen and farmers continued to use traditional measurements, such as the *shaku*, the common distance measurement of about 30 cm (Hashimoto 1998, 202). The trees in this block are spaced at the uneven English distance of 19.68 feet but exactly at the round distance of 20 *shaku* apart. It seems likely that the design of this garden employed traditional Japanese forms of measurement in laying out what might otherwise look like an American-style alignment of trees.

Based on the artifacts located in this garden (especially the marbles found there), the residents of this garden would have spent time together under its shade trees. The cohesive garden design along the entire length of the building also made a strong visual statement of connectedness. Because this garden ran the length of a barrack, it is likely that a number of residents were involved in its creation and maintenance, but historical research has uncovered a likely leader in the design of this space (Hawley 2016). Among the six households in this barrack, only one was occupied by a professional gardener. Issei Denzaburo Kishi and his family lived in unit 11H–1E. The War Relocation Authority (WRA) case files indicate that Kishi was a gardener, information confirmed by census research. In both the 1930 and 1940 US Censuses, Kishi is shown in Los Angeles, with his occupation listed as a gardener working in private homes. As such, Kishi would have had extensive experience maintaining and likely designing yards and gardens.

The sophisticated melding of two traditions in the 11H roadside garden is the kind of design we would expect to see from someone with Kishi's experience. It could have been informed by experience in modernizing Japan, with its innovative blending of traditions. But this garden also exemplifies scholar Kendall H. Brown's (1999, 13) contention that for many Issei, "building gardens served as a way of defining their Japaneseness and of maintaining ties to the homeland left behind, but also as a means of securing a living and even assimilating into their new country." As such, Japanese-style gardens in North America are always Japanese American, part of a "hybrid culture based on layers of transmission and appropriation" (9).

The 11H roadside garden is notable in part because it is something of an anomaly. Many of the public gardens are located more toward the center of barracks blocks, areas with greater internal access by the residents. The layout of the buildings in each barracks block was the same, with barracks flanking two central public buildings. While the mess hall was always adjacent to the road, behind the combination laundry/latrine was a fairly large open space lying between the two rows of barracks buildings. In a number of blocks, this public area was claimed by young people, who pressed it into service for sports and other games. Indeed, in some blocks there were developed facilities in this location, such as leveled fields, baseball backstops, or basketball courts (figure 6.6).

The first archaeologists to survey Amache noted the presence of walls in the public area of Block 9L (Carrillo and Killam 2004). The full extent and shape of these walls, however, was obscured by soil and surface vegetation. I

FIGURE 6.6. Historical photograph of baseball backstop in Block 12K. Detail of panoramic photo taken by Jack Muro.

chose to investigate this area during the first field season at Amache, hypothesizing that these walls might be part of a public garden. Before starting our field work, my crew chiefs and I explored these features further, pin-flagging all the visible wall segments. This low-tech form of visualization helped us realize that this area was likely once graced by a pair of rather extensive oval garden beds. This was the perfect scenario for the use of ground-penetrating radar (GPR). As discussed in chapter 2, GPR is a non-invasive way for archaeologists to be able to "see" below the surface of the ground. In this case, we wanted to test our supposition that these features were garden beds before investing the effort required for excavation. GPR would quickly let us know if the visible portions of the walls were continuous below the surface. It would also reveal if these walls were the surface manifestation of a pond, because the concrete bottom of a pond would affect the radar very differently than a bed filled with soil. The GPR results revealed two oval features of exactly the same size, both of which were filled with sediment (figure 6.7), strongly supporting our hypothesis about these features serving as garden beds.

The next step was to more thoroughly investigate these features through excavation. This was to be the first garden excavation at the camp, and our

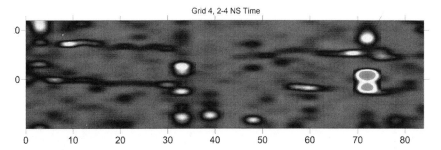

Grid 4, 2-4 NS Time

FIGURE 6.7. Ground-penetrating radar slice map of oval garden indicating the location of walls, stepping stones, and other buried features. *Courtesy*, DU Amache Project.

research design was strongly shaped by ethical commitments to site stewardship. Rather than completely excavating any garden, DU Amache crews always dig only a portion. Doing so preserves much of the gardens for the future, in part in the hope that later archaeologists will have even more sophisticated analytical techniques than we do. Choosing strategic areas of gardens to test is also a more efficient use of time and resources. For the 9L garden, we chose to investigate the west garden oval, in part because the GPR had revealed another likely feature associated with the bed. Crews began by carefully revealing the entire oval wall, which would allow more exact placement of our test units. Subsequently, we carefully laid out our grid in a way that divided the bed in half along its long axis. Arranging our test units in a checkerboard along that grid meant we could assess the symmetry or asymmetry of the interior elements within this very geometric garden bed.

Our strategy was successful. Excavations made it clear that whoever designed the Block 9L garden features was not strictly adhering to traditional Japanese garden design. There is an almost unnerving symmetry in the design of the 9L garden beds; indeed, they seem much more like a European garden than a Japanese one. To start, the beds themselves are perfectly oval, the same size, and oriented in accordance with the gridded layout of the block's buildings. Excavations in the west bed revealed the remains of a tree planted exactly on the centerline of the bed, a design decision highlighting the symmetry of the beds themselves (figure 6.8).

In another innovation, the material for the garden walls was cinderblock scavenged or taken from stores of camp construction materials. Excavations

FIGURE 6.8. Photograph of 9L oval garden excavation. Note the remains of the tree in the center of the bed. *Courtesy*, DU Amache Project.

revealed how each block was carefully split into three portions and laid in a way that disguises the block's defining features—its circular center holes. Without rather close inspection, the pieces appear to be carefully quarried basalt blocks, a material that would have been familiar to any of the dozen professional gardeners who lived in this block.

Despite what appears on the surface to be a very Westernized design, the Block 9L garden was still informed by Japanese landscape principles. One of the most influential of these is *shakkei*, which literally translates to "borrowed scenery." Many of the gardens at Manzanar appear to be sited to draw the eye to particular mountain peaks (Helphand 2006, 184). The location of Amache on the High Plains affords fewer such opportunities. Still, the camp sits on a terrace slightly higher in elevation than the Arkansas River, so from a few places one can see the trees that line the riverbank. To the northeast also lies the small town of Granada, visible from 9L because the block juts out east of all the other barracks blocks. Although not as majestic as the Sierra, the borrowed scenery of this Amache garden would have been reassuringly civilian. The importance of places that provided respite from the military landscape of camp is hard to overstate. Jeanne Wakatsuki Houston (1973, 72) recalled that in the Manzanar gardens, facing away from the barracks, you could "for a while not be a prisoner at all."

The plant remains recovered from the 9L ornamental garden are as intriguing as its design. We recovered enough of the tree to identify it as *Ulmus pumila*, or Siberian elm. Near the planting hole we identified a square stain in the soil that was likely from a decayed wooden stake. We also recovered a length of copper wire, a material restricted to military use during the war. Like the cinderblock in the garden, it suggests that someone in this block had access to the stores of camp construction materials. The wire and decaying stake together indicate that the tree was staked out for stability or perhaps to be trained into a particular shape. Either strategy would have helped it better thrive in the windy High Plains. We also recovered high concentrations of *Portulaca*, or purslane seeds, in the soil samples from the oval garden. This strongly suggests that *Portulaca*, a weedy plant found around the world, may have been deliberately grown as an attractive and drought-tolerant ground cover. As noted by Steven N. Archer (2009, 5), archaeobotanist for the Amache Project, "*Portulaca* does not seem to have tremendous significance in Japanese gardening traditions, but as abundantly evidenced elsewhere, Amache incarcerees were adept at substituting or being inventive with local materials, including plant materials."

Our investigations in the gardens of 9L exemplify the productive synergy of archaeological research done in collaboration with a community of living memory. We were very fortunate that our first field season was punctuated by a conference on internment held in Denver. I was able to gather with conference attendees who had been at Amache, listening to their recollections and sharing some of our results. One incarceree I checked in with was Minoru Tonai, who had been a resident of Block 9L. Minoru's recollections were ones I would later hear echoed by others who lived in this block. With a large population of young adults used to the bright lights of Los Angeles, 9L was known throughout camp as a party spot, a reputation reflected in its nickname, "Chinatown." The location on a high spot and a bit away from the other blocks meant that music played at night in 9L would carry to the other blocks in camp.

With visions of "Chinatown" in my head, I returned to the 9L garden excavations. The very next day my crew discovered a bottle of bright red fingernail polish in the garden. Mr. Tonai had specifically mentioned that a number of the Nisei women in the block had been waitresses in the city and were much more cosmopolitan than women the same age who hailed from small towns or family farms. It was easy for the crew and me to immediately envision one of the worldly ladies of 9L sitting in the garden painting her nails such a scintillating color.

Our work has revealed other activities that fed into Block 9L's lively reputation. It is clear that the parties in this garden involved drinking a range of beverages, including alcohol. Intensive survey of the block in 2012 revealed the remains of at least one and perhaps two saké jugs at the base of a tree located between the latrine and the garden beds. A concentration of lightbulb glass fragments there suggests that the tree had lights, probably run from the electricity in the nearby building. Lights in that tree would have illuminated the garden area, something that would also have been visible to other blocks.

At the Amache reunion in 2009, I was fortunate to meet Benjamin Tani, who also lived in Block 9L with his family. He seemed to recall that his older sister's scrapbook had pictures of the 9L gardens and was gracious enough to send me scans of them afterward. Several of the photographs (one of which is included here as figure 6.9) show friends and family posed in front of the west oval bed, the one we had excavated the summer prior. The tree whose roots we had recovered is evident in the right-hand side of the photo. The picture also clarifies the location of a gazebo or shade structure that Minoru Tonai had recalled being located somewhere in the block. Many photos in the 9L scrapbook show kids in gardens, and the garden as a space for families is also supported by the archaeological evidence. One of the first artifacts we recovered from the garden was a small plastic barrette in the shape of a butterfly. Historical photographs of little girls in camp show them wearing a range of similar hair accessories. The oral histories, photographs, and excavations combine to reveal that the 9L garden probably had two different lives—one peopled by families with children who enjoyed it during the day, and one of younger adults, playing music and imbibing, in the evening.

FIGURE 6.9. Amache servicemen on leave before deployment photographed in front of the 9L garden with friends and family, 1943. *Courtesy,* Benjamin Tani on behalf of the Tani family.

As is clear from the 11H and 9L excavations, block gardens brought people together. It would have taken considerable work to create the hardscaping, plant the trees, construct features like a gazebo, and care for the plants. People of all ages seem to have enjoyed the gardens, and as our investigations revealed, a wide range of activities took place there. Such communal gardens helped block residents reweave the ties of community unraveled by the process of removal and incarceration (Kamp-Whittaker and Clark 2019).

The Amache Park

It is likely that all ten of the WRA confinement camps had public gardens or parks of one sort or another. Undoubtedly, the most famous is Manzanar's Merritt Park, in part because both Ansel Adams and Dorthea Lange photographed it during the war. Covering an acre of land in what was originally

FIGURE 6.10. Block managers pose in the 6H garden adjacent to their office. *Courtesy*, Amache Preservation Society, Granada, CO.

a fire break, Merritt Park centered on a strolling garden complete with a pond and a teahouse. It was designed by brothers Akira and Kuichiro Nishi and supported by the WRA, which paid the construction crews at the high end of the camp wage scale—between sixteen and nineteen dollars a month (Helphand 2006, 186).

The public gardens at Amache were much more modest in scale. The garden best known to visitors, both historically and currently, is the hill-and-pond garden in Block 6H. The recreation hall, named the Amache Town Hall, in this block housed the central office for all of the camp's block managers. As befits a park next to the seat of local government, it was a showpiece for the camp. It served as the backdrop for photographs of camp dignitaries (figure 6.10) and was generally a popular locale (Nishizaki 2011). Some of our best evidence for the composition of this garden comes from the photographs of Jack Muro, a devoted amateur photographer who lived in a barrack nearby (Ono 2013). Jack photographed the garden (and people in it) at many different times of the year (figure 6.11).

FIGURE 6.11. 6H garden decorated with paper lanterns. *Courtesy,* Jack Muro, photographer.

By combining photographic evidence, oral histories, and close examination of the remaining physical fabric, a fairly robust picture of the garden can be ascertained. Its central design elements were paired: a figure-eight–shaped pond and an artificial hill. These elements were linked with a curved wooden bridge, which spanned the pond (figure 6.12). Hill and pond features have their roots in the strolling gardens of the Edo period but are typical elements of Japanese-style gardens in the United States. Both the pond and the hill make significant use of large rounded river cobble, which was gathered from the terraces of the Arkansas River. As in the 11H garden, its designers employed large upright rectilinear pieces of concrete formed by the pouring of barrack foundations. These pieces were used both in the center of the hill and in the pond. Two such "standing stones" were paired with plantings to create islands in the lobes of the pond. The pond still bears circular impressions left by round wooden posts that once lined its edges, a common design technique called *rangui*. Taken as a whole, the design of the 6H garden was harmonious, beautiful, and almost stereotypically "Japanese."

A close look at the lower left-hand corner of the photograph in figure 6.10 reveals what appears to be an electric lamp of the kind often used in shops or

FIGURE 6.12. Historical photograph of 6H garden from 1998 calendar prepared for an Amache reunion. Annotations by Kazie Yoshida Aoiki. *Courtesy,* Amache Preservation Society, Granada, CO.

outdoor settings. It likely tapped into the electrical system of the Town Hall. In figure 6.11 we see more temporary paper lanterns. Both types of lighting would have made the garden visible and more welcoming at night. Another of Jack Muro's photographs captures some of the more whimsical elements in the garden, especially a pair of birdhouses, one of which is clearly marked "6H" (figure 6.13). The detail revealed in these photos—hand-carved wood and the tin cans used to secure the birdhouses to their posts—displays the combination of care and ingenuity common in the arts and crafts of Amache (Swader 2015). Evidence of the community's attachment to this garden goes beyond its design and use: a lovely sketch of the garden in the scrapbook of a woman who lived in 6H as a teenager shows that she, too, was inspired by this locale (figure 6.14).

Several students and I were fortunate to have the opportunity to meet Fumiye Nishizaki, who lived and worked in Block 6H. In speaking with us

FIGURE 6.13. Birdhouses in 6H garden. *Courtesy,* Jack Muro, photographer.

FIGURE 6.14. Drawing of 6H garden from the scrapbook of one of the block's residents incorporating a photograph taken by Jack Muro, another block resident. *Courtesy,* family of Joy Takeyama Hashimoto and Jack Muro.

(Nishizaki 2011), she recalled how her husband, Tomotaro, worked with the block managers who met in the Town Hall. He took the minutes for the daily meetings and reported to the project director, James Lindley. Fumiye also worked in the Town Hall, where among other tasks she coordinated the use of the block's sewing machine. Because of the couple's jobs in camp, Fumiye had an insider's view of the construction of the garden outside Town Hall. She noted that the people involved in its design had expertise in gardening; indeed, seven block residents were enumerated by the WRA as having worked previously in gardening professions. These gardeners, however, were far outnumbered by those involved in agriculture in general; over sixty of them lived in 6H, and Fumiye recalled that many people worked very hard to make the Town Hall garden come to fruition. For example, much of the hardscaping material for the garden came from the Arkansas River, especially the river cobble. Each stone would have had to be gathered, loaded into a truck, unloaded, and then set into concrete. Fumiye noted that it took several trips with a camp truck to transport all of that river cobble. Although on current maps the garden is often called a *"koi* pond," Fumiye was clear that the fish in the pond also came from the Arkansas River. As such, they might have been either catfish or carp, the latter of which is related to *koi.*

A few other clues about the construction of this garden can be found in the holdings of the Amache Preservation Society Museum. These include materials related to the reunions of former Amacheans and their families. Among these collections is a commemorative calendar featuring a historical photograph of the 6H garden (see Figure 6.12). Under the photograph is this note, handwritten by former incarceree Kazie Yoshida Aoiki (1998): "My father Mr. Haruichi Yoshida and many other men, women, and children all helped to make this pond in our block, 6H. Seeds were ordered from the Sears Roebuck catalogue and also the Montgomery Ward catalogue." In 1940, Haruichi Yoshida was a farm laborer living with his family in a rental house in Turlock, California (US Bureau of the Census 1940). Block 6H was largely composed of families from the Central Valley of California, including the area of Turlock. Like Mr. Yoshida, the majority of those who helped construct this garden had experience in agriculture but were not landscape professionals.

Mr. Yoshida's story and Mrs. Nishizaki's recollections highlight some similarities and differences between the construction of the Block 6H garden and that of Merritt Park in Manzanar. In both instances there was at least some support from the WRA, but at Amache it was restricted to the use of a camp truck and likely access to construction materials, such as the concrete for the pond. Both parks make use of local stone in designs strongly influenced by pre-war Japanese American public and commercial gardens (Brown 1999); however, the Amache garden reveals a much more vernacular flair. It was not designed by a known landscape architect, it appears no one was paid for their work on the garden, and rather than plants from a nursery, many of the plants were propagated from mail order catalog seed.

In 2014, we discovered additional evidence of just how well used and appreciated the 6H garden was while the camp was occupied. That year we investigated features in the central area of Block 7H, which is immediately south of Town Hall. There we identified a likely central garden during survey, and we excavated portions of a foundation that once supported a traditional Japanese bath (*ofuro*) (Haas et al. 2017). Ground-penetrating radar (GPR) prior to excavations showed a possible linear feature running north toward 6H. Subsequent test excavations in the area of the GPR feature revealed a pathway smoothed and compacted by foot traffic. Trees were planted at points along the pathway, and fragments of lantern glass recovered in excavation suggested that it may have been illuminated at night. The pathway led directly from the amenities in the public area of 7H to the 6H garden.

Perhaps even more than individual block gardens, the creation and maintenance of the park next to Amache Town Hall required a significant investment of time. Because it was associated with the managers of every block, it is likely that people from across the camp helped construct it. Certainly, it was something people throughout Amache were engaged with, as revealed both in historical photographs and in the pathway from Block 7H. By creating a showpiece traditional Japanese-style garden, Amacheans made a statement not just to themselves but also to site visitors. They might have been incarcerated because they were Japanese, but they were not turning their backs on the aesthetics of their heritage. Just the opposite: they were employing their skill and art to good effect on the High Plains of Colorado.

The Nation and Diaspora—Victory Gardens

During World War I, leaders encouraged civilians of all stripes to grow food either on their own land or in common areas. Powered by the slogan "food will win the war," the Victory Garden movement helped relieve wartime food shortages without funneling more land and labor into established agricultural enterprises. In World War II, the Victory Garden movement was quickly re-energized. Historical catalogs of the type incarcerees may have used to order plants echoed the government propaganda of the era. As the

FIGURE 6.15. American flag made from vegetables at the Amache Agricultural Fair, September 1943. Historical photograph by Joseph McClelland. Government document available on Calisphere.

president of the Salzer Seed Company proclaimed in his introduction to the January 1942 catalog, "Mother Earth and Guns Will Maintain Democracy: Food will be our mainstay" (Salzer 1942).

Amache participated in the Victory Garden movement with enthusiasm and in some instances displayed that investment to outsiders. One of the primary methods for showing off the residents' engagement was the Amache Agricultural Fair, held the first fall after the camp opened. This event was the Amache equivalent of the county fair, with hundreds of people outside the camp and thousands within it participating (*Granada Pioneer* 1943f). The patriotic messages carried by these wartime gardens are clearly captured in photographs of the fair (figure 6.15). Articles about the fair in the *Granada Pioneer* make it clear that the vegetables grown in camp were cast in such terms. Among the competitive entries were those in the "victory garden" category, which allowed entry by individual, block, and school class (*Granada Pioneer* 1943g).

Although the irony of gardening for victory in an incarceration facility was likely not lost on the adults of the camp, it was still a powerful metaphor, especially for children. Cohorts of school kids—elementary, junior high school, and

FIGURE 6.16. Amache children working in their class victory garden, June 1943. Historical photograph by Joseph McClelland. Government document available on Calisphere.

senior high school—were assigned plots in the camp's farm program for their own victory gardens (figure 6.16). Their efforts were encouraged by the camp staff and administrators, including the cartoonists for the *Granada Pioneer*. A recurring feature of the paper was the cartoon character Lil' Neebo, created by former Disney cartoonist Chris Ishii and continued by other cartoonists after he joined the United States Army (Asakawa 2012). Lil' Neebo's name is shorthand for "Little Nisei Boy," and his name suited him; he was wildly popular among the children of the camp. The first spring at Amache, the cartoon featured Lil' Neebo in his victory garden (figure 6.17). A student-written article in the junior high school newspaper documents some of the plants the students grew, including carrots, lettuce, squash, and radishes, the latter of which were a favorite for students to eat in the garden. Revealingly, the article goes on to state that the gardens will make the students healthy in two ways: "because of working out of doors in the garden, and also from having the vegetables to eat" (Horimoto 1943, 1). An editorial by a ninth grader makes it clear that at least some students understood the political ramifications of their work in

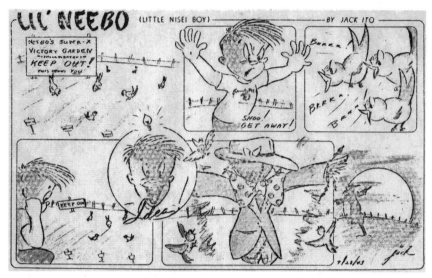

FIGURE 6.17. Lil' Neebo victory garden cartoon from *Granada Pioneer* (April 28, 1943). *Courtesy*, Japanese Americans in World War II Collection, Special Collections Research Center, California State University, Fresno.

the gardens: "If we all get out there and work for our rights, and our lives, we may be able to make these United States a better place for the Japanese to live in. There are farms large enough for everyone to work on. We may raise vegetables, poultry or cattle, or may even drive tractors. Our tanks and trucks and planes run on gas, but we run on our stomachs. So let us supply this land with food until victory is won" (Sakaguchi 1943, 2).

In addition to the official victory gardens set aside on the farm, historical photographs document a number of victory gardens located along the edges of barracks blocks and other common areas. These larger gardens seem to have served as something akin to community gardens, and they were likely located throughout Amache. Some of those vegetable gardens were tended by former farmers, including those in Block 12E, which was among the blocks at Amache with the greatest concentrations of agriculturalists (over seventy). Those farmers almost certainly contributed to their block's award-winning victory garden entry in the Amache Agricultural Fair (*Granada Pioneer* 1943g).

Some of the best photographs of victory gardens were taken from the water tower on the southeastern corner of the camp. These photos document how the gardens of Block 12K, adjacent to the water tower, evolved over time

FIGURE 6.18. Historical photograph of 12K VG-1 garden taken from the camp's water tower. Joseph McClelland photograph. Government document available on Calisphere.

(figure 6.18). The 12K gardens were tended by far fewer residents who had worked in agriculture or horticulture. Only thirty in total lived in that block; unlike 12E, the majority of them (twenty) were in the gardening professions.

In 2008, crews tested one of the 12K gardens (designated VG-1, or victory garden 1) because we could firmly connect the garden to its original location in the block. Unfortunately, this garden yielded no definitive macrobotanical evidence of what had been grown there. The pollen results were more promising, which is sometimes the case in such circumstances because pollen survives longer in the ground than do seeds (especially large, uncharred ones). We recovered pollen from four different plant families that are often grown for food or as ornamentals (Jones 2015). Appropriate to a vegetable garden, one of these was pollen from the *Brassicaceae* family, which includes cruciferous vegetables such as cabbage. Bok choy, or Napa cabbage, known in Japanese as *hakusai*, is an important Japanese staple that is commonly pickled or used in a number of dishes. We also found pollen from the Sumac family (*Rhus*), which can be both an ornamental and an herb. Strictly ornamental plants are reflected in pollen of the primrose family (*Onagraceae*) and *Dalea*, which is a type of flowering legume. Wild varieties of each of these plants do grow in the area, and the pollen may derive from native plants. All four of these plant families are insect-pollinated, which leads to more limited production and dispersal of pollen grains. Thus they are likely to have been growing either in or near the garden.

In addition to the plants likely grown there, excavations in VG-1 revealed gardening strategies employed by those who worked this plot. Both as we were excavating and in the screen, we found many pieces of small-diameter white tubing, which was likely associated with how this garden or individual plants within it had been watered. Our excavations also revealed an alignment of moderately circular features consisting of finely textured sediment that was much darker than the surrounding matrix. A return to the historical photograph with an eye to interpreting these features revealed a line of plant pots running through the garden (see figure 6.18). When these were watered, moisture would have escaped through the bottom drains of the pots, taking some of the darker, richer soil in the pots with it. These circles of darker soil, as well as fragments of terra cotta pots that we recovered, were the archaeological markers of this practice. Analysis of the soil chemistry in the garden suggests that the whole plot was not subject to soil amendment, but these features show that the gardener(s) were strategically using pots that held better soil for some plants. The resolution of the photograph is such that without the excavation data, it is unlikely that we would have been able to identify this practice from historical evidence alone.

In 2010, Amache site managers were planning to return the original camp water tower, which had been discovered in a nearby farmer's field through tireless research by local advocates. Much of the original tank could be reused, but the tower itself was to be reconstructed. As noted above, good photographic evidence for gardens in the vicinity of the water tower existed because of the photographs taken from it. To ensure that reconstruction would result in as little impact as possible to Amache's archaeological resources, we conducted studies in the vicinity of the tower. In particular, we wanted to keep construction activities away from the victory gardens.

As noted earlier in this chapter, in 2008, GPR in the 9L oval garden had been quite successful. In comparison, our investigations of gardens with less hardscaping (stone or concrete) had been less successful. So in 2010 we refined our GPR methods. To better capture the relatively shallowly buried and often ephemeral garden features of the camp, we shifted to more fine-grained GPR analysis. Woody vegetation (such as sagebrush) was cleared to allow for better coupling between the antenna and the ground surface. We

FIGURE 6.19. Historical photograph of victory garden (VG-2) in Block 12K (bottom of the image). *Courtesy*, Amache Preservation Society, McClelland Collection, Granada, CO.

also switched to a different type of antennae, one that better captures near-surface phenomenon (a 400 mhz rather than a 900 mhz), and we ran transects at a very close, 25 cm spacing.

Our results were very promising and helped us protect the southernmost garden in Block 12K (designated VG-2). As can be seen in historical photographs, the edges of this garden were demarcated not by hardscaping but by a wooden fence (figure 6.19). Despite this fact, the boundaries of the garden, especially the corners, were distinct in the GPR reflections (figure 6.20). Test excavations in this garden revealed intact remnants of a light wood fence, the slats held in place with wire. It ran in the same direction as the GPR reflections and appears to have been their source (Clark, Garrison, and Swader 2012). With these studies, we had identified the far corner of the garden and were thus able to mark it off and protect it during the tower reconstruction.

Another great success that year was our soil chemistry analysis of the garden. Unlike the victory garden to the north, VG-2 had a strong chemical signature of care for the soil and the plants in the garden. When compared to control samples, the garden levels of the excavation units (those associated with fence remains) revealed elevated levels of ammonium nitrate, phosphorous, and potassium (Marín-Spiotta and Eggleston 2012). These nutrients

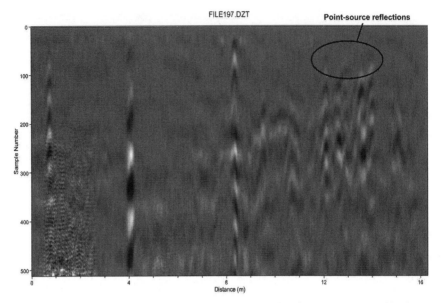

FIGURE 6.20. GPR profile revealing the 12K VG-2 garden fence as a series of high-amplitude point-source reflections. *Courtesy*, DU Amache Project.

assist in the growth of plants and are commonly found by archaeologists researching fertilized soils (Miller and Gleason 1994). Soil pH levels for this area were also more neutral than is typical at Amache (Marín-Spiotta and Eggleston 2012). The soil pH and the abundance of useful nutrients reveal the care with which incarceree gardeners improved the camp's poor soil.

As with the 2008 garden, little in the way of seed or plant remains was recovered, and we were again more successful with our pollen results (Jones 2012). We recovered pollen from the potato family, indicating that potatoes were likely one of the plants grown in this garden. A greater surprise was to find pollen from *Canna*, a tropical plant originally from South America and now grown in many areas, including Japan. *Canna* is primarily decorative and typically grown from rhizomes (lilies and iris are also propagated that way). Historical catalogs suggest that *Canna* would have been available to order; however, the *Canna* at Amache may have followed a different route to camp.

Hawaii is a tremendously important locale in the Japanese diaspora. Many of the immigrants who eventually made their way to the US mainland first immigrated to Hawaii. There, they typically worked on plantations, becoming familiar with the traditions of their co-workers, including Native Hawaiians. With support from my university, I traveled to Hawaii researching historical, archaeological, and garden sites throughout the islands. My explorations and conversations with local experts confirmed that *Canna* grows wild in Hawaii, especially on sites where there was once a significant Japanese population. For example, wild stands of *Canna* grow at the Kahuna Gardens in Maui, once a plantation, and are often seen growing at Japanese Hawaiian coffee farms throughout the Kona Coast of the Big Island. With a number of important exceptions, people of Japanese ancestry in Hawaii were not incarcerated on the mass scale they were on the mainland. Family or friends of people at Amache would have been free to gather Hawaiian resources like *Canna*. While in Hawaii, I met with Japanese American families with a connection to the mainland camps, including Kay and Edwin Kaneko. Kay (then Uno) was incarcerated at Amache but afterward moved to Hawaii. Edwin had lived in Hawaii his whole life. My conversation with the Kanekos (2013) and other Japanese American families in Hawaii suggests they helped out as much as they could during the war. People, for example, sent things to the camps (Kaneko and Kaneko 2013).

The *Canna* grown at Amache might have had another connection back to Hawaii. Although it is not an indigenous plant, *Canna* has become important in hula. The plant's beautiful black seeds are used in *uli uli*, a type of gourd percussion instrument employed by many dancers or by musicians who accompany them. Hula is an important tradition of the Japanese Pacific diaspora. People from Japan, as the Kanekos (2013) suggested to me, are drawn to hula because it also expresses Japanese values. The Amache newspaper reflects that hula and other Hawaiian-themed entertainment was common in camp. A number of performers, notably Diane "Bubbles" Endo, often danced to music by Brush Arai and his band, the Kanaka Boys. A program for a "Rhythm Show" held in the spring of 1944 indicates that one of the three acts for the night was devoted entirely to Hawaiian song and dance (Unknown 1944). The *Canna* grown at Amache would have enlivened the victory garden in 12K with beautiful blossoms, but it might also have been used, along with gourds, to create *uli uli*. Given the importance of other traditional crafts in camp, this remains a tantalizing possibility.

Facing displacement and war, Amacheans recreated connections through gardening. As explored in this chapter, some of those connections were made

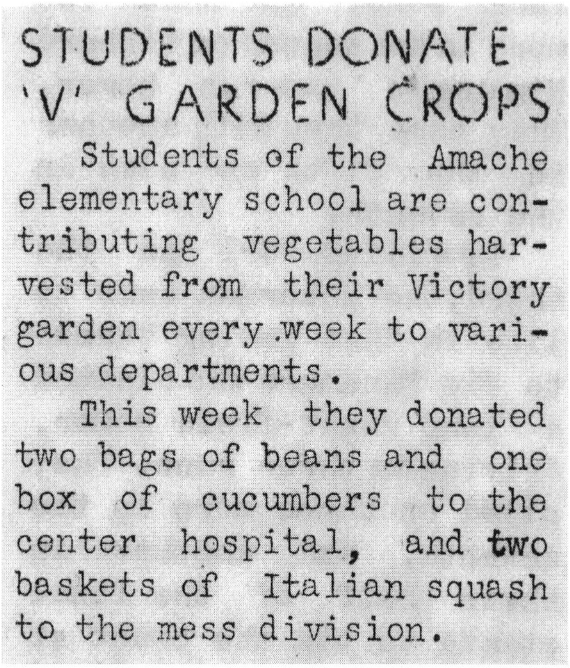

STUDENTS DONATE 'V' GARDEN CROPS

Students of the Amache elementary school are contributing vegetables harvested from their Victory garden every week to various departments.

This week they donated two bags of beans and one box of cucumbers to the center hospital, and two baskets of Italian squash to the mess division.

FIGURE 6.21. *Granada Pioneer* article about the distribution of school victory garden crops (August 4, 1943). *Courtesy*, Japanese Americans in World War II Collection, Special Collections Research Center, California State University, Fresno.

at home. By growing nutritious produce that could be turned into familiar dishes, Amacheans took care of themselves and their families. This was just one of many practices through which the women of the camp reclaimed their traditional roles as caretakers (Shew 2010). The work of creating and maintaining these gardens tied families together as well, as kids pitched in to dig and water. Likewise, the creation of gardens in individual blocks like 11H and 9L would have brought people with different skills together. Scavenging for the range of materials found in these gardens likely drew from the ranks of those employed in different areas of the camp. Once established, these gardens provided a place for families and friends to relax in a much less militarized setting than the rest of the camp. In the case of the garden next to the Amache Town Hall, that setting was also an important locale for connecting to the outside world. Visitors to the camp even today are drawn to the elegant lines of the hill-and-pond garden there.

Those connections lengthen to the global scale in the victory gardens. By casting their vegetable gardens as "victory gardens," the incarcerees engaged in an international dialogue about patriotism through plants. This happened across the generations: while parents grew food for their kids, children were lauded for the contributions their victory gardens made to the success of camp operations (figure 6.21) (*Granada Pioneer* 1943h). Cynically, one could suggest that these families, many of whom would end up with children in the service, had already given more than their fair share to the war effort. And yet, even the simple act of growing potatoes was another way they proved their commitment to winning the war. But the victory gardens, like all the gardens at Amache, are complicated. By including plants of the Japanese diaspora, such as *Canna*, these gardens reveal enduring global connections. Indeed, one could argue that each of these gardens—through the plants grown, their overt design, and the underlying philosophy—was indelibly Japanese American.

7

Tradition and Innovation

Historical photographs of Amache consistently capture images of tiny garden after tiny garden adjacent to its barracks. Although the site has good
examples of larger gardens, it is at the small scale of the entryway garden
that Amache makes the greatest contribution to a broader understanding
of how incarcerees transformed the landscape of all ten War Relocation
Authority (WRA) camps. This is in part because of good site preservation
but also because that intact landscape can be tied to camp directories; thus
we can easily connect these entryway gardens to the people who made or
enjoyed them. Photographs suggest their ubiquity, but six summers of intensive archaeological survey and test excavations have further revealed the
diversity and complexity of these small, everyday spaces (figure 7.1a, 7.1b).

Typically, an entryway garden flanks either side of a barrack doorway,
which would have served two different living units. The gardens often had
some type of border, whether fencing or stone outlines, and many incorporated shade trees. Close examination goes beyond these generalities to reveal
a wide variety of gardening tastes and techniques. The gardens' similarities

DOI: 10.5876/9781646420933.c007

FIGURE 7.1a.
Example of entryway
gardens—historical
photograph. *Courtesy,*
Amache Preservation
Society, McClelland
Collection, Granada,
CO.

FIGURE 7.1b.
Example of entryway
gardens—current
photograph. *Courtesy,*
DU Amache Project.

and differences speak to the many ways these raw areas adjacent to living spaces became a canvas upon which Amacheans expressed both traditional values and diasporic aesthetics.

As noted in chapter 6, strolling gardens—with water features, bridges, and stone lanterns—are likely the type of Japanese-style garden with which most Americans are familiar. But in Japan, the gardens with which people interact on a more daily basis are *tsuboniwa*, or courtyard gardens. The term derives from a unit of measurement, the *tsubo*, which covers an area about 10 feet

(3.3 meters) square. Smaller varieties of the *tsuboniwa* would have taken up a space of between three to four *tsubo* (Itoh 1973). That is comparable to the space in front of the barracks at Amache.

In many ways, the courtyard garden derived its inspiration from the gardens created outside of teahouses (Itoh 1973). Both are informed by architecture, and both can be used as a passageway from one space to another. Not all courtyard gardens in Japan are meant for moving through; rather, some are viewed exclusively from the outside. Some of the key hardscaping elements of *tsuboniwa* in Japan are stepping stones, lanterns, and water basins (Itoh 1973). Plants are also critical. They can run right up to the building and either create interest in or hide architectural elements. An overgrown look created by overlapping plantings gives the impression that the building was placed in a landscape that has always been there (*House Beautiful* 1960). Such gardens softened the division between building and landscape. Perhaps most important, a garden in one's living and working space enriched the home environment, bringing art and beauty to daily life.

Another critical influence on these entryway gardens was the cultural landscape of the United States. From the Victorian era onward, social critics, developers, and the popular media emphasized that American families should live in houses surrounded by yards (Schroeder 1993). Certainly, not all Amacheans would have lived in this setting, but it was an ideal to which they would have been exposed. This is particularly true of the 205 incarcerees whose pre-war occupations were coded as "gardeners and groundskeepers" or as "housemen and yardmen." The 40 Amacheans whose occupations were "nursery operators and flower growers," along with children and wives involved in family nurseries but uncounted by the WRA, also would have influenced the kinds of plants that ended up in these yards. Indeed, the front yards of the Pacific states owed some of their flair to the talents of their Nikkei residents. The entryway gardens at Amache are hybrids, an adaptation of the American front yard with roots in the *tsuboniwa*.

Passing the Time—the Gardens of 12H

Before their incarceration, most Issei had very little free time. In no small part because of institutional racism, even most college-educated Japanese immigrants started their American work lives as manual laborers. Working long, physically taxing hours left little time for leisure pursuits. Yet once behind barbed wire, many incarcerees, especially older Issei, had too much time on their hands. Both the incarcerees and the administration understood that to be a problem. As a result, both WRA-sponsored and incarceree-driven activities—including sports, arts and crafts, adult education, and performances—flourished.

Gardening was one activity that could be pursued to pass the time in camp, and the records kept by the War Relocation Authority for Amache provide insightful context.[1] Among the forty-one summer activities for students and adults at Amache High School was the garden club. Institutional support of gardening also came in the form of books about gardening in both the junior high and senior high school libraries, like one titled *Rain in the Garden*. The administration also supported a "parent-school relationship" lecture series at the high school complete with Japanese translators. Among the offerings was an excursion titled "Plants: sage, cactus, yucca, flowers, grass, seed" (WRA n.d.). Other documents, however, suggest some tension around the resources needed for gardening. *The Pulse* (1943, 12), a magazine supplement to the camp newspaper, includes an article called "Amache in Retrospective" in which the author notes: "Many blocks are planting Chinese [*sic*] elms around the barracks and some people are making small garden plots even though the administration warns them of the lack of water. Maybe those people prefer a bit of green to a shower in the summertime."

As with Denzaburo Kishi, discussed in chapter 6, some of Amache's gardeners were professional horticulturalists, and their gardens were a reflection of their pre-camp work lives. But by combining historical records with the physical remains of the camp, we have established that many of our most interesting entryway gardens were created by individuals who may have gardened only at Amache.

Block 12H was occupied almost entirely by individuals from Los Angeles. Two such households were those of Saichiro and Bun Hirota, who lived in

---

1 Many documents produced by or under the auspices of the War Relocation Authority were kept by the National Archives and Records Administration (NARA). They are classified as Records Group 210. Those items were subsequently microfilmed, and the films are available at many libraries or for purchase. The reels that pertain specifically to Amache are classified as "field documentation" and are FILM B 3062, Reels 44 through 55. All of the items cited in this paragraph are among the microfilmed documents.

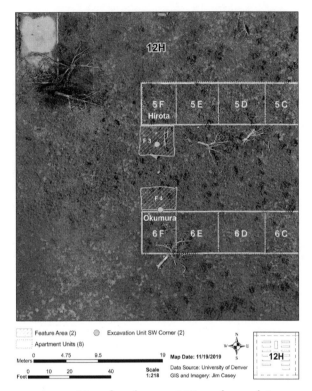

FIGURE 7.2. Map of gardens at 12H Barracks 5 and 6 surveyed and tested by DU Amache crews. *Courtesy,* Jim Casey.

12H–5F, and Chozaburo and Ai Okumura, who lived directly south of them in 12H–6F (figure 7.2). These neighbors were similar in many ways. They were older Issei living alone, and both couples had been merchants in Los Angeles prior to the war; the Hirotas were grocers while the Okumuras ran a hardware store.

The aesthetics of these neighbors' gardens, however, could not have been more different. While the Okumuras' garden is decidedly traditional, the Hirotas created an inventive entryway garden that made use of nearly every material available in camp. Crews discovered the Hirota garden during pedestrian survey in 2010, when a student noticed a water pipe placed vertically into the ground, collar up. It appears, especially from a distance, like a plant pot set into the ground. Ground-penetrating radar suggested there were even

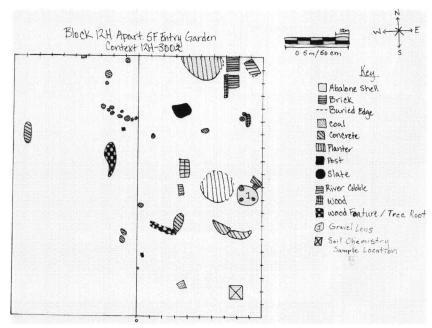

FIGURE 7.3. Map of Hirota garden based on excavation data from summer 2010. *Courtesy*, DU Amache Project, inked by Emerson Klever.

more intact portions of the garden, and so we opened up an excavation unit there. When crews cleared off the surface vegetation, a second pipe emerged closer to the barrack entrance. Further excavations revealed the corner of what was likely a brick landing at the doorway. They also clearly indicated that the upright water pipes had indeed been used as planters and that their placement was very deliberate: the pipe planters are in an alignment at a 90 degree angle to the barrack, marking the east edge of the garden. A second alignment of materials to the west emerged from the excavation and included a wide variety of materials—imported stone, rounded cobble from the Arkansas River, an outsized piece of coal (figure 7.3). The hardscaping elements are eclectic overall but are laid out in a very linear fashion.

A number of plants were likely grown in the Hirota garden. Excavations revealed the decaying in situ (in its original location) remains of the base of a tree (Clark, Garrison, and Swader 2012). Although it was too decomposed for us to identify the species, a tantalizing hint comes from the pollen remains.

Analysis of samples taken from the garden revealed the presence of *Prunus*, a family that includes cherry, plum, peach, apricot, and almond, along with a great variety of ornamental species (Jones 2012). In addition, we recovered pollen from the decorative shrub, dogwood. Since the pollen from these species does not travel far, they were likely deliberately cultivated in this garden.

After clearing off the loose surface soil deposited by the wind since the camp was abandoned, crews discovered a light but consistent scatter of carefully crumbled eggshell within the garden. The soil filling the pipe planters was also similarly amended. One person who was not surprised that we had discovered eggshell in the garden was Kay Uno Kaneko, who along with her daughter and granddaughter came to visit us at Amache. Kay recalled that eggshell, as well as tea leaves and coffee grounds, were all highly prized soil amendments; however, not everyone had access to them—you had to know people who worked in the mess halls.

Well-drained arid soils like those at Amache typically have low levels of calcium, so the Hirotas counteracted that deficiency through soil amendment. The eggshell in their garden would have raised the calcium level in the soil, thus creating a more nutrient-rich environment for plants. Our soil chemistry analysis bore this out, with the planters and the garden strata containing two to three times more calcium than was found in our non-garden control plots (Marín-Spiotta and Eggleston 2012). Crumbled eggshells can also deter pests like slugs and snails.

Although we did not choose to do test excavations there in 2010, both surface and GPR survey that year suggested that another garden was located in front of the barrack facing the Hirotas. In 2014, we opened a test excavation in the garden in front of 12H–6F where Chozaburo and Ai Okumura lived, in part to understand the correspondence (or lack thereof) with the landscaping of neighbors (Kamp-Whittaker and Clark 2019). What crews found was a strikingly different garden from that of the Hirotas.

The primary design element of the Okumura garden is a series of larger "stones," each a piece of concrete likely salvaged from site construction projects (figure 7.4). One stood near the entryway, with another alignment running at an angle toward the barrack. This creates a loosely triangular space adjacent to the barrack. It quickly became apparent that within this triangular area had been a consistent layer of small (1–2 inch diameter) gravel, almost certainly gathered at the Arkansas River (Haas et al. 2017). No planting

FIGURE 7.4. Okumura garden after excavation, summer 2014. *Courtesy,* DU Amache Project.

holes were discovered, but a few fragments of terra cotta pots suggested that some plants had been grown in the garden. That supposition is supported by the recovery of pollen from ornamentals including phlox, cockscomb, globe amaranth, lily, and prairie coneflower. One sample had particularly high numbers of *Asteraceae*, a family of plants widely represented in the local wildflowers (Haas et al. 2017).

This variety of ornamental flower stands in somewhat stark contrast to the hardscaping of the garden, which comes across as a traditional *karesansui*, a dry garden of gravel surrounding larger "stones." In Japanese gardens (most notably in Zen monasteries), this combination is used to evoke a seascape; the larger stones are individual islands and the gravel represents water (e.g., the Sea of Silver Sand garden discussed by Holborn [1978, 53]). It is likely that the Okumura garden was composed of different zones, one of which was a dry garden, while at least one area contained ornamental plants. Indeed, the gravel concentration thins out increasingly the farther it is from the standing elements.

In April 2015, I was honored to discuss our research with attendees at an Amache reunion (the second in which I participated). In particular, I enjoyed talking informally with former incarcerees who were generous enough to spend some of their precious reunion time with me and my students. Over dinner, two women who had been young girls in camp mentioned that they had lived in Block 12H. Sumie Maruya Domoto shared that at Amache she learned to play the *koto*, a traditional Japanese stringed instrument, from none other than Ai Okumura. She also recalled that Chozaburo Okumura had been involved in productions of traditional Japanese theater performed in their block's mess hall. Delighted at the serendipity, I ran to find pictures of the Okumura garden to share with Sumie. She was pleased but not surprised to see what we had recovered; both Mr. and Mrs. Okumura, in her words, "were very refined" (Sumie Domoto, personal correspondence 2015). Clearly, this couple had deep knowledge of Japanese traditions, knowledge they used in many ways to improve life at Amache.

The Okumura and Hirota gardens faced each other and both served to enliven the otherwise drab landscape, but their differences call out to us more than seventy years later. They point to how individualistic, almost idiosyncratic, the gardens at Amache could be. The Okumura garden was very traditional, a garden that even today is identifiably in the Japanese style. It was arranged in such a way as to counterbalance the strict symmetry of the barrack architecture, a technique advocated by Japanese garden designers (Hayakawa 1973, 166). The elements of the Hirota garden, in contrast, aligned with the barracks at right angles. In its overall layout, it feels much more like an American front yard. However, the incorporation of eclectic, reused materials leans across the Pacific toward Japan. Although the earliest Japanese palace gardens largely emphasized natural materials, later Zen practitioners often incorporated cast-off artifacts in their garden design. Some of them, like lanterns from abandoned Shinto shrines, were chosen to bring *sabi*, or a sense of timelessness, into the garden. But others were more quotidian, with an eye to the beauty overlooked in everyday objects. In fact, the writings of both Zen philosophers and tea masters chided gardeners for spending money on exotic elements when perfectly suitable items were near at hand. Both subscribed to an "aesthetic philosophy to discover new value in things that had been abandoned as worthless" (Itoh 1973, 83). Although less aesthetically "Japanese," the Hirota garden nonetheless derives from some of the same values that shaped their neighbors' garden. Indeed, both families drew creatively on the possibilities of cast-off materials, the detritus left from camp construction. By utilizing

FIGURE 7.5. Mataji Umeda in his garden, from his granddaughter's Amache scrapbook. *Courtesy*, Helen Yagi Sekikawa.

leftovers in their works of art, both the Hirotas and the Okumuras employed a philosophy both aesthetic and spiritual.

Gardening Farmers

The 12H entryway gardens were discovered during survey, but others have been identified using historical photos of known locales. Several of my students and I were also able to attend an earlier Amache reunion, held in 2009. Many attendees brought scrapbooks of photos and other memen tos from camp. While paging through Helen Yagi Sekikawa's scrapbook, I was immediately struck by the photos of a very ornate entryway garden, many featuring a distinguished elderly gentleman (figure 7.5). That man was Mrs. Sekikawa's grandfather, Mataji Umeda. She kindly allowed us to scan all of her photographs there at the reunion. The following field season, spurred in part by the interest of graduate student David Garrison, my crews and I went in search of Mr. Umeda's garden.

Mataji Umeda, his wife, Hatsuye, and his youngest child, Toki (who like Helen was a teenager in camp), lived together in Block 7G at Amache. Like most of the residents of this block, before the war, the Umedas lived in the northern Central Valley of California. Mr. Umeda was a tomato farmer with a talent and passion for growing chrysanthemums (Sekikawa 2013). The historical records are somewhat in conflict regarding where in Block 7G the Umedas lived. The 1945 directory indicates that they were in unit 5F, while the 1943 directory places them in unit 6F. It was not uncommon for incarcerees to move within the camp, especially as better housing opened up. Mrs. Sekikawa recalled her grandparents living in 6F but not 5F. One might be tempted to dismiss the association with 5F as a typographical error (which it very well could be), but a database compiled by my students using both camp directories indicates that no other households were associated with either unit 6F or 5F.

The archaeological data only complicate the picture. Crews doing intensive pedestrian survey of Block 7G encountered extensive hardscaping in the area of unit 6F. In fact, unlike most gardens, the one at 6F actually wraps around the barrack, an arrangement Mrs. Sekikawa recalled for her grandfather's garden. The historical photos of the Umeda garden indicate that it incorporated a pond, as does the garden in front of 6F. We also noted a large, non-local stone present in the space in front of 5F. To further investigate the area, we set up a ground-penetrating radar grid between Barracks 5 and 6, but we had to avoid the extensive hardscaping of the 6F garden feature, for two reasons. First, we did not want the antenna to damage the extensive garden elements. Second, many of those elements stood significantly above the current ground surface; running the antenna over them would have created an "uncoupling" with the ground and prevented our acquisition of data about features below. We were, however, able to successfully use our GPR equipment to explore the area in front of unit 5F, and the data suggested we might find buried garden components. So we opened up two excavation units in front of 5F: one where the GPR suggested we would find garden elements and another adjacent to it to explore the extent of the garden.

The GPR revealed point reflections in an alignment, as one might expect from stepping stones. As excavators began to remove the topsoil, some river gravel and a number of pieces of dimensional cedar lumber were revealed (Clark, Garrison, and Swader 2012). Cedar is not a kind of lumber used in the construction of the barracks, so we were intrigued by its presence in the excavation unit. Soon, the source of that lumber became clear. The point reflections were each standing cedar posts, still in situ in the garden (Garrison 2015). The fact that they were part of a garden fence was made all the more obvious when a horizontal piece of lumber between the two posts was recovered. Crews also recovered a good number of different types of wire, including copper wire, from this unit. A rationed material during the war, wire may have been part of the fence construction, or it could have been used to support or train plants.

The soil samples revealed some of the plants that were likely grown in this fenced garden. Samples from the fence posthole held high quantities of High spine *Asteraceae* pollen. Sunflower, daisy, and zinnia are among the ornamental cultivars of this family. Their pollen rarely travels far distances, which suggests that these plants were deliberately grown in the historical garden (Jones 2012). Zinnias were particularly popular at Amache; at the 1943 agricultural fair, an entire section was devoted to their display (*Granada Pioneer* 1943g). Crews who floated the soil from this garden recovered purslane (also known as moss rose) seeds, a decorative ground cover, and mustard family (*Brassicaceae*) seed that is either peppergrass or tumble mustard (Archer 2012).

Whether Mataji Umeda had a hand in this garden remains something of a mystery. When we compare his granddaughter's recollections and the photographic evidence to what we discovered through site survey, it does appear that 7G–6F was the Umeda family's primary residence. However, it is also possible that Mr. Umeda—whose garden there wrapped entirely around the barrack—would have landscaped an otherwise blank expanse across from (and thus visible from) his own extensive garden. That might explain why the family is associated with 5F in the camp directory. Regardless, our work in the 7G–5F garden was decidedly fruitful. It taught us that a garden that was otherwise completely undocumented historically and revealed only by the most minimal evidence on the surface (in this case, a piece of non-local stone) could be accurately predicted through GPR. In fact, an overlay of the excavation unit findings and the GPR suggests that even fairly subtle features, in this case, wooden posts, are quite clear in the reflections (Garrison 2015, 50–51).

The garden at 7G–5F is another expression of Japanese American aesthetics. The wooden fence that cordoned off the garden followed the linear geometry of the barracks rather than having a more asymmetrical design. The simple post and rail fence was one that would be equally at home in a Japanese garden and an American front yard. One of the most striking elements of the

FIGURE 7.6. Quartz from surface of the 7G garden. *Courtesy,* DU Amache Project.

garden, the one that alerted us to its possibility from the surface, is a large piece of quartz (figure 7.6). During excavation we found an even larger exotic stone, a piece of petrified wood, in situ in the garden. As noted in chapter 2, employing unshaped stone in gardens is one of the earliest Japanese garden traditions. Some of the earliest garden specialists in Japan were the "stone-setting" priests of the Shingon sect (Hayakawa 1973). Setting stones was a specialty because it needed to be done very carefully. Without thoughtful consideration, it would be easy to upset the stone's spirit (or in Shinto terms, its *kami*). As the Sakuteki admonishes, in garden design it is important to "follow the request of the stone" (Takei and Keane 2001, 4).

The lengths to which the gardener who created this space had gone to procure these stones only became apparent once we were back in the lab. Very specific geological conditions are required for wood to become fossilized, and the nearest source of the petrified wood is an outcropping of the Morrison geological formation in the vicinity of La Junta, Colorado, about

70 miles east of the site. But the quartz had an even longer journey. The 7G–5F garden stone is a specific form of quartz—pegmatite—that forms in the cracks of igneous or metamorphic rock. Although such stones are sometimes transported by water, the sharp edges of this stone indicate that it was likely collected near the source. Quartz of this type is commonly found in the Rocky Mountains, far west of Amache. Oral histories note that some of the Christian teenagers at Amache attended a Bible camp in the foothills of the Rockies (DU Amache 2011). Perhaps someone associated with that trip noticed the striking stone and brought it back to camp. While concrete could (and often did) do in a pinch, it would never have the *kami* of a stone found in nature.

The Bachelor Gardeners of Amache

At the turn of the twentieth century, the Japanese gardeners of Southern California were often former domestic workers drawn to a profession with plentiful opportunities and few startup costs. By building on that early start, what had been an underdeveloped industry was by 1920 "an ethnic niche and by WWII, a near ethnic monopoly" (Tsukashima 2000, 69). Many of these gardeners were single men who lived together in boardinghouses that could serve as combination employment agencies, prefectural organizations, and training facilities. Indeed, they came to be known as "gardeners' colleges" (Tsukashima 2000), an appellation applied to the Domoto nursery discussed in chapter 5 (Riggs 2013).

In 2012, we discovered a garden associated with two bachelor gardeners in front of Barrack 9 in Block 11H, the same block as the roadside public garden discussed in chapter 6. Although obscured by blown soil, a linear feature of vertical concrete pieces and a possible stepping stone were identified there by survey crews. The feature's location was particularly intriguing; it was placed directly in front of the barrack doorway, a configuration unlike any other entryway gardens we had previously identified. Following our research protocol, the next step was GPR (see figure 2.4 for an image of crews doing GPR in this garden), which suggested that the alignment was more extensive under the ground surface and perhaps associated with other landscaping.

Excavations in this garden revealed two additional concrete stepping stones and several nearby planting holes. It also became clear that the concrete

FIGURE 7.7. Close-up of prickly pear impression and angling of wall pieces in 11H entryway garden, summer 2012. *Courtesy,* DU Amache Project.

pieces barely visible on the surface were the top of a carefully designed wall. Like the stepping stones, the flat concrete pieces employed in the wall appear to have been poured for use in this garden (rather than the by-products of camp construction, as seen in many other gardens). Each concrete element of the wall was set into a base of crushed limestone. The wall pieces are angled into the ground, and the overall effect is that of a miniature mountain range. One piece of the wall has a distinctive impression in the concrete. After staring at it for several days, the student excavating that portion of the wall suddenly recognized the shape: a prickly pear cactus (figure 7.7).

As excited as crews were about the garden wall, they were about to uncover something even more surprising. I was overseeing excavations in

FIGURE 7.8.
Walkway and wall
in 11H entryway
garden as revealed in
summer 2012 excava-
tions. *Courtesy*, DU
Amache Project.

another part of the site when my walkie-talkie crackled with a message from the garden crew chief; I needed to head his way immediately. In a unit we had opened up between the wall and the barrack, the excavation crew had revealed an alignment of cedar lumber placed into the ground surface at regular intervals parallel to the barrack foundation. They suspected that this was a walkway leading from the barrack doorway directly to the garden wall. Their suspicions were confirmed once they uncovered a cedar plank delineating one edge of the walkway (figure 7.8).

The seventy-year-old pieces of lumber were quite fragile, so excavations in the area proceeded slowly and with great care. Much of the time, the crew dug this feature from outside the unit so as not to crush the wood (figure 7.9)

FIGURE 7.9. Student excavating in 11H entryway garden. *Courtesy*, DU Amache Project.

because our goal is to reveal gardens, not destroy them. Yet to understand what was grown, garden elements do sometimes need to be moved, if temporarily. I was keen to know if there had once been some kind of ground cover grown in the spaces between the wooden elements of the walkway. One piece of wood was a bit askew, so we decided to excavate down beneath it. That way we could carefully remove the wood, take a pollen sample from underneath, and then replace it when we were done. In attempting to take the sample, the crews discovered that what we had thought were smaller pieces of lumber making up the majority of the walkway were pieces of lumber the same size as the 2 inch × 8 inch plank delimiting its edge. These pieces were placed with the thin edge deeply set into the ground, so excavating below the plank could have undermined the physical integrity of the entire feature. We stopped the excavation at that point, but it was not without benefit, for it showed us exactly how the walkway had been constructed (Driver and Clark

2015). These deep planks stabilized the walkway better than would have been the case if more narrow lumber had been used. Especially given the site's sandy soil, this was a smart, if labor-intensive and more expensive, decision.

A pollen sample taken from underneath a small stone jammed between two walkway slats suggested that some of the plants that might have been grown in the garden included members of the rose, nightshade, and sumac families. Most notable were grains of mint (*Lamiaceae*) pollen (Jones and Williams 2015). Mint pollen is poorly distributed, so the plant was likely growing very near the spot where we recovered its pollen. Some species of mint are used in Japanese-style gardens in the United States (for example, at the Denver Botanic Gardens) as a type of ground cover. The presence of mint pollen in this location may indicate that it was planted between the slats of the walkway.

Because of the extensive nature of this garden, we took many soil and pollen samples, which revealed a wide variety of plants that were grown in or near the garden (Jones and Williams 2015). From the planting holes, we commonly recovered pollen from corn, *Prunus* (cherry, plum, peach), and *Rhus* (sumac). A single grain of *Apiaceae* may reflect the presence of parsley in the garden. Multiple soil samples revealed a number of *Portulaca* seeds, which may have derived from either the wild or the domesticated variety. Pollens associated with the lily, mallow, and blackberry families consistently appeared throughout other samples. A surprise, because there didn't appear to be a water feature in the garden, was the recovery of cattail pollen.

Soil samples taken from the general garden area revealed multiple petunia seeds (Archer 2015). A popular flower during the 1940s, petunia seeds would have been easy to procure from a number of mail order catalogs. Also intriguing was the recovery of many seeds from the *Kallstroemia*, or caltrop, family. Caltrop, a low woody plant with small attractive flowers, is native to the region of Amache. As noted by the project archaeobotanist, they "may represent another instance of locally available plants being tended in a garden context" (Archer 2015, 177). Finally, in a single sample we recovered pollen from locust and clover (*Trifolium*). Clover pollen is only removed from the flower by insects. The presence of *Trifolium* pollen in this sample suggests that clover flowers decomposed within the garden. Finally, analysis of phytoliths revealed that *Canna*, noted in chapter 5 as a common plant in Hawaii, was also found in this garden.

The 11H entry garden was complexly woven together with many different plants and hardscaping elements. That complexity also extends to its soil. One of the benefits of taking soil samples is that microartifacts and other human-introduced elements that would otherwise be lost during screening can be recovered. That is because when soil is processed in a flotation tank, not only do we collect the "light fraction," plants and other organic remains that float to the top, we also collect the "heavy fraction," the items that sink to the bottom. Because the water breaks up soil structure, we can employ much smaller mesh than we use in our dry screening; through flotation, we recover anything larger than the mesh of a window screen. Students rarely relish having to sort through heavy fraction because it's mostly just little fragments of rock. However, if they have a good eye for detail, they might discover something fascinating.

Such was the case for one student, who along with all the others enrolled in my Historical Archaeology class in the fall of 2012 was tasked with sorting the heavy fraction from that summer. Jessica Gebhard (2015)—whose master's thesis focused on editorials in the *Granada Pioneer*—noticed that some of the heavy fraction from her 11H garden soil sample looked like slightly rusty metal. Among the larger grains of sand were tiny pieces of iron, but looking at them with a magnifying glass revealed that they were not the expected broken-down bits of tin can or wire. These tiny artifacts had the rough surface and irregular shape of slag, the melted bits of metal that result from blacksmithing. Elemental analysis of the alloy in one of the largest pieces confirmed our suspicions. Although it was not magnetic, it was 96–99 percent iron. The loss of magnetism is related to how it has been treated; it occurs in iron heated to very high temperatures.

After Jessica's discovery, the other students in the class were on the lookout for similar items. Sure enough, in every single soil sample from that garden, students found more pieces of slag. Inspired by her discovery, Jessica did more research and discovered that concrete (the material for all the barracks foundations) leaches iron out of soil. By carefully introducing tiny pieces of slag throughout the garden, its makers had helped produce the sort of environment in which all those plants could thrive. We found a few pieces of iron slag years later in the Barrack 1 garden in 11H. It seems likely that someone in this block had connections to the Amache blacksmith shop located on the cattle ranch outside the central camp area.

FIGURE 7.10. Tub of fish harvested from the Arkansas River by Amacheans. This still was captured from a 16 mm movie made at Amache. *Courtesy*, Amache Preservation Society, Tsukuda Collection, Granada, CO.

The Barrack 9 gardeners used more than iron to improve the soil. In processing the light fraction, archaeobotanist Steven Archer also discovered two small fish bones. Fish products were an important soil amendment in Meiji era Japan (Hayami 1964), and the nearby Arkansas River would have been a source for such fish. A particularly interesting Amache home movie shows groups of older men using a large net to catch fish. Most of them are small enough that they would have been difficult to process for eating but would have been perfect for making fish meal or fish-infused compost tea (figure 7.10). Gathering, processing, and mixing both the iron slag and the fish remains into the soil are yet more parts of the pattern of the garden. This space was created with care and maintained with diligence.

Such a garden comes about only through expert knowledge and skill. I was not surprised when one of the crew, doing additional archival research on the garden she was excavating, discovered that it was associated with professional gardeners. The doorway integrated into this garden design served two barrack units in 11H: 9E and 9F. WRA documents indicate that 9E was occupied by Zenhichi Sairyo and Kashichi Yokoi, men who had been employed as gardeners before the war. Subsequent research suggests that both of their names were misspelled by the WRA and are likely Zenkichi Sairyo and Kahichi Yokoi, respectively.

Like most other residents of the block, these men were from greater Los Angeles. Mr. Sairyo is noted on his 1912 draft registration card as a gardener for the Los Angeles Railway Company (US Selective Service System 1912). In the 1930s he appears in a Los Angeles directory as the manager of a nursery (Ancestry.com 2011). Mr. Yokoi's 1918 draft registration indicates that he was a farmer in Stockton, California, but by 1940 was running a cactus nursery in Los Angeles (US Selective Service System 1918; US Bureau of the Census 1940). After discovering this fact, I thought back to the prickly pear cactus impression in the wall of the garden. Knowing that one of these men had made his pre-war living growing cacti adds resonance to this design choice.

The birth (1885 and 1886, respectively) and immigration dates (1914 and 1915, respectively) of Sairyo and Yokoi are strikingly close, and both were unmarried. They clearly had much in common, and it is likely no accident that they came to share a living unit at Amache. Their ages and dates of immigration also fit the demographic profile of many Issei who were employed in the Los Angeles area as professional gardeners. Indeed, such men often shared accommodations before the war, in part because they were unmarried.

Sairyo and Yokoi would have possessed the skill sets and formal training necessary to create this garden. Their backgrounds as Issei meant that they undoubtedly would have been exposed to traditional Japanese landscapes and perhaps even gardening practices before they left Japan. Their experiences in the United States—farming, gardening, running nurseries—would have deepened their horticultural knowledge. The two men's similar life experiences and living situation could have bonded them together, a connection likely deepened through their shared project—this remarkable garden.

When the camp was occupied and the many plants of this garden were at their peak, the space would have exhibited many of the characteristics of the *tsuboniwa*. It was lushly planted and employed stepping stones. The

mountainscape created by the concrete pieces was an example of a miniaturized landscape of the kind sometimes employed in viewing gardens. In
overlapping the pieces in the wall, Sairyo and Yokoi followed a centuries-
old technique for creating depth and evoking mountains (Slawson 1987, 116).
Another way to bring larger elements into small gardens is through *shakkei*. Although it is commonly thought of as a technique for framing distant
views (like mountains or forests), *shakkei* can also bring in nearby elements
(Hayakawa 1973, 140). The impression of the prickly pear cactus in one piece
of the concrete wall ingeniously employs a normally utilitarian material to
this aesthetic end. By capturing the cactus in the concrete, the gardeners
could bring that element to their garden without incorporating a potentially
hazardous plant in a space traversed many times a day.

Channeling movement in and out of the barrack is a defining trait of this
garden. Yet the carefully created pathway from the barrack door leads not to
a clear exit but to the garden wall. Although only partially excavated, lumber
discovered in situ leading to the right side of the wall suggests there might
have been a secondary pathway around that edge. There was another way
around, as on the left was a series of stepping stones. Tea gardens likewise
channel movement along a *roji*, or pathway, but not one that leads directly
to a destination. They often meander and employ various barriers. These
designs slow movement and encourage mindfulness, a key function of both
Zen practice and the Way of Tea. Although this garden did not lead to a
teahouse, it served a similar purpose for all who traversed it by making them
pay attention to their surroundings.

The Entryway Gardens of Amache

Over millennia, gardeners in Japan experimented with a range of techniques
grounded in various religious and philosophical traditions, from Shintoism
and Confucianism to Buddhist philosophy and the Way of Tea. By the Meiji
era, which launched the first emigrants to the United States, Japanese gardening coalesced into a coherent set of philosophy and practices for revealing
nature within spatial limitations (Hayakawa 1973). Gardens were such a key
element of Japanese domestic architecture that homes were defined by "a
unity of room and garden" (Hayakawa 1973, 144). Indeed, the Japanese word
for family, *katei*, when written in the traditional character script of kanji,

is formed through a combination of the characters for house and garden (Denoon and McCormack 1996).

The heart of the Japanese garden is natural scenery. As Masao Hayakawa (1973, 166) suggests, this can take three different forms in the garden: nature in miniature, elements of a natural scene, and nature as abstracted. At Amache we see all of these different forms employed in the entryway gardens. Some expressions of nature are more obvious, like the miniature mountains of the 11H–9E / F garden and the tiny bridge and pond created by Mataji Umeda. Amache's high desert setting made copying familiar natural scenes difficult. But by employing *shakkei* and securing striking stones, gardeners brought elements of nature into their gardens. Finally, the Okumuras evoked an abstracted seascape in their garden, a soothing counterpoint to the guard tower that loomed over the barrack (see figure 7.4).

Plant selection is another way Japanese gardens can be rooted in nature. Early Japanese gardeners would transplant wild specimens; the gardening guide *Sakuteiki* suggests that in particular, old trees should be sought out (Takei and Keane 2001, 167). As Kenneth I. Helphand notes, incarcerees at many of the WRA camps returned to the practice of using nature as a nursery. The result can be seen in the Joshua trees at Manzanar and the pruned sagebrush at Minidoka (Helphand 2006). At Amache, our botanical studies reveal how practitioners used a wide variety of native plants in their gardens, from water-wise ground cover like purslane to local wildflowers like caltrop. Some gardens employed cactus either as the primary design feature or complementing other elements (figure 7.11). Like the stones that graced gardens, some of these cacti came from nearby, but others were collected from further away. During survey we discovered a particularly striking garden in Block 9L with a small pond, a lovely bluish stone, and cholla—a tall, lanky variety of cactus (figure 7.12). While taking photographs of this garden, I was visited by a local rancher who often comes to the site to check in on the crew's most recent finds. Unprompted, he pointed to the cactus and said, "That doesn't belong here." Cholla, although common in other areas of Colorado, doesn't grow in the immediate environs of Amache (and if there's one thing ranchers know about, it's cactus). This plant was collected some distance from camp.

Many of the materials employed in the Amache entryway gardens were not traditional but were innovations that took advantage of what gardeners

FIGURE 7.11. Historical photograph of an entryway cactus garden at Amache. Note also the homemade wheelbarrow in the background. Crews recovered a similar homemade wheel during site survey in 2010. Photograph by Joseph McClelland. Government document available on Calisphere.

FIGURE 7.12. 9L entryway garden with cholla, a variety of cactus that does not grow in the vicinity of Amache. *Courtesy,* DU Amache Project.

FIGURE 7.13. Entryway garden tree surrounded by broken tile paving. *Courtesy*, DU Amache Project.

had at hand. The Hirota garden—with its broken pipe planters and alignment of coal, brick, and stone—is a notable example. Another favorite was discovered by crews during survey in 2010. David Garrison (2015), whose thesis focuses specifically on entryway gardens at Amache, brought me over to see a feature in Block 12K. He and his crews had noted a concentration of broken tile surrounding a tree and wondered if this was yet another type of entryway garden design (figure 7.13). Impressed by their keen observation skills, I asked, "Have you seen any other concentrations like this *not* in a garden?" In fact, they had not, and we observed together how carefully the tile was spread and how it surrounded the tree like paving. In the end, we were all convinced that this was not a dump but was indeed a design.

The reuse or adaptation of materials by incarcerees was a significant strategy for improving life in camp and, as noted earlier, one with roots in Japanese gardening traditions. This value was expressed concisely by one of our 2016 volunteers, Greg Kitajima, a professional gardener whose mother and other family members were incarcerated at Amache. In an interview about the camp gardens he noted, "They were so limited in what they had . . . the use of concrete slabs is reflective of the Japanese American spirit" (cited in Gómez 2016).

Cases where gardeners employed items that were otherwise trash appear to be a manifestation of the traditional Japanese value of *mottainai*, the idea that waste is shameful. It is a stance that draws from both Shinto and Buddhist beliefs regarding the respect one should pay to the spirit inherent in physical things (Sasaki 2006). Another crew chief, Paul Swader (2015), studied the recycling of materials at Amache for his master's thesis. His work not only links the practice to the camp landscape but also highlights how it shaped the arts and crafts made at Amache, for example, wood carvings and furniture made from shipping crates. Evidence of this frugality-based aesthetic has also been documented at other camps, where cast-offs served as critical raw materials (Eaton 1952).

The ways *mottainai* shaped practices of the Nikkei community are explored by Lawson Fusao Inada, a poet who as a young boy was confined first at Jerome in Arkansas and then at Amache. In "Harry from Hiroshima," Inada writes of a worker who carefully saves shipping materials from the fish shop where he and the narrator work. The worker, Harry, goes so far as to straighten out the nails pulled from shipping crates. When he accompanies the narrator to the town dump, Harry reacts negatively, calling out repeatedly, *"Moht-tai nai"* (Inada 1997, 85). So although the materials in Amache's gardens are innovative, they draw from traditional values as well, ones that had also served the Japanese American community well before camp as they struggled through the Great Depression. What is so striking about the Amache gardens are the many ways this value translated into aesthetically satisfying and imaginative design.

But not all the items some gardeners desired were available through scavenged or scrounged materials. For example, many of the entryway gardens incorporated cedar lumber, a material not available in camp. Likewise, although some of the trees and plants found in these gardens were gathered and transplanted, many others were purchased from local nurseries or as seeds from catalogs. These items, and the gardens in which they would be employed, were valued enough that they were purchased with funds often depleted by the upheaval of removal. Indeed, the administration noted in one report that the cultivation of entryway gardens took place at incarcerees' own expense and time (WRA 1943a, 6).

Crews are often visited in the field by both tourists and local residents. Toward the end of our 2010 field season, a former mayor of Granada spent the day watching us work in the 7G entryway gardens. He had often visited the camp as a boy and so had a personal interest in our results. When I asked if he remembered gardens at the camp, he replied that he absolutely did. In fact, he declared, Amacheans had created something magical here. The camp, he recalled, was beautiful. He repeated himself for emphasis, "It was beautiful here." Many, many words have been used to describe Japanese American incarceration facilities, but "beautiful" is not generally one of them. Yet I had to agree with him. In these small gardens, Amacheans created strikingly humane spaces all the more remarkable because of the inhumane place in which they were planted.

8

Placemaking in Confinement

A primary task any archaeologist faces is to notice patterns in the material traces of human behavior and then try to explain them. Over the course of six seasons of archaeological research at Amache, one of the most robust and seemingly mysterious patterns is the ubiquity of gardens. When one envisions a military incarceration facility, gardens aren't the first phenomenon that comes to mind. And yet, in every single block occupied by the Japanese Americans incarcerated at Amache, archaeology crews have uncovered gardens of different sizes, composition, and complexity.

As discussed in chapter 3, the archaeology of Amache's landscape was shaped by a number of research questions. What my crews and I have found in pursuing those questions is woven throughout this book. Some of the questions were easier to answer, like whether gardens existed in areas of the site to be impacted. But for others, the answers continue to unfold, constantly refined with each new season's discoveries. In trying to answer the question of how these gardens fit into the picture of life in confinement, one must contend with their sheer number. The fact that there are so many of

DOI: 10.5876/9781646420933.c008

them—that they are the rule rather than the exception—is critical to understanding what role they might have played.

To help answer the question of why there are so many gardens at Amache, one can turn not just to the literature on confinement but also to interdisciplinary theories about how and why people make places. Placemaking is one of the rare, truly universal human practices. As anthropologist Clifford Geertz (1996, 262) wrote, "No one lives in the world in general." Instead, our lives are interwoven with places, which shape our actions and thoughts, house and arouse our memories, and serve as group and personal identifiers. Archaeologist Barbara Bender (2002, S110) suggests that we pay attention to the human processes involved: "The unfolding of place is part of the unending performance of social life."

The most obvious expressions of placemaking are physical changes to the environment, and archaeologists see them across the globe and through time. Such modifications take a wide variety of forms, ranging from the stacking of stones along a trail to art painted in caves to the building of urban centers. Managing natural resources is often a key factor, with water storage, the harvesting of wild plants, and the selective burning of landscapes activities that predate the construction of architecture. But the process needn't require physical changes. As ethnographies of mobile groups suggest, placemaking can happen through naming, an act that not only imbues locales with time depth but also allows people to anchor their histories and stories in space (Basso 1996).

Why are places so important? At the most basic level, they meet physical needs. People need shelter and food and water, and places provide that. But our physical selves and our psychological selves are connected. Each of the places where your life happens—the kitchen, the school yard, the church—becomes a part of who you are. They are interwoven into your routines, the stories you tell, indeed, your very sense of self. Imagine the disorientation when connections to those places are lost. To be whole, people in those situations have to reclaim the self through remaking places. Anthropological studies of migrants (Law 2005) and the homeless (Zimmerman and Welch 2011) confirm that even in temporary locations, the urge to create new places, to personalize our surroundings, is very strong.

The energy poured into the gardens at Amache is not just the making but the enriching of places to a surprising extent. Is something deeper at play? Historically, Japanese gardens were sacred space and gardening was a spiritual act. The gardens at Amache likely echo this, meeting not just the physical and mental but also the spiritual needs of incarcerees.

Meeting Physical Needs

Gardens effectively combatted one of the most pressing environmental problems at the camp, which was the relentlessly blowing sand. A by-product of the site's location on the High Plains, the soil on which it was built, and its method of construction, the problem was both a daily occurrence and, in times of sandstorms, acute. Combatting the gritty wind was the primary rationale the students gave in their plea for gardens at the elementary school. There were other widespread landscaping efforts in incarceree barracks blocks as well. Minoru Tonai recalled that in his block, 9L, people banded together to plant front lawns. All along his barrack building (number 3), residents planted drought-tolerant rye grass. They then dug a ditch around the beds to keep the water in. However, the War Relocation Authority (WRA) established water restrictions soon thereafter, and much of the grass died (Tonai 2011). Survey in 9L revealed widespread evidence of entryway landscaping (figure 8.1). Indeed, we only saw one pair of barrack buildings that were not fronted with evidence of gardens, but they have several trees. Perhaps, like the Tonai family's barrack, the other landscaping was more like a lawn, which without hardscaping would be difficult to see seventy-five years later.

Landscaping not only helped keep the dust down, it also tempered the often hot and arid climate of Amache's high desert setting. The hundreds of shade trees incarcerees planted at Amache are perhaps the most obvious intervention, but there were others. As suggested by our soil chemistry analysis and as recalled by several former incarcerees, these gardens required constant watering. Our investigations have discovered several clever water management techniques, including possible soaker hoses and large tin cans modified to be plant pots (figure 8.2). Still, much of the time, plants would have needed to be watered frequently, and our soil chemistry analysis suggests consistent spot-watering in gardens (Marín-Spiotta and Eggleston 2012). The evaporative cycle from such watering would have tempered the low relative humidity of the areas immediately adjacent to barracks. The many ponds we've discovered during survey would have done so even more effectively.

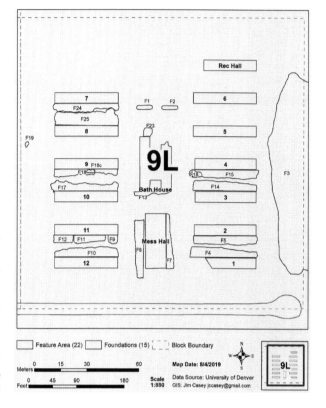

FIGURE 8.1. Map of features discovered during survey of Block 9L. Almost all of them (except for the F3 trash scatter) represent gardens or other landscaping features. *Courtesy,* Jim Casey.

Growing foodstuffs was another important way camp residents helped meet their physical needs. Among the products of Amache's agricultural program were some traditional Japanese crops, including daikon, mung beans, *gobo* (burdock root), and tea (Simmons and Simmons 2004, 27). In victory gardens, Amacheans had even more control over their diet by choosing which plants to propagate.

The health benefits of fresh produce, however, are just one of the ways gardens can contribute to the health of the body. Those readers who are gardeners know that gardening is a very embodied practice. Much of the work involves bending over or squatting, repeatedly. In the spring, preparing beds can be quite a workout, especially in vegetable gardens, which need to be dug up each year. In the summer one needs to start early, before both worker and plants are wilting in the sun. Although some aspects of gardening, especially landscaping, can feel a bit like weightlifting, yoga is the more apropos

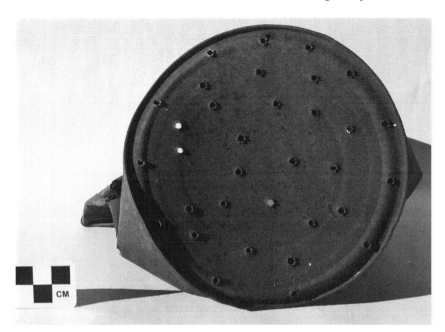

FIGURE 8.2. Tin can turned into a plant pot at Amache. *Courtesy*, DU Amache Project.

parallel. Like yogic practice, some of Amache's gardens were designed to induce mindfulness, but one does not just meditate on or in gardens—one also meditates *through* gardening. One modern gardener describes her experience with establishing a community garden and orchard as "a Zen exercise in mindfulness, discipline, and the joy of being right in the moment . . . gardening at its best is an exercise in being connected to the rhythms and vibrations of daily life" (Wann 2003, xii).

The reality that a healthy garden requires constant attention is one of the reasons they work so well in this capacity. And although we cannot know if Amache's gardeners worked in them regularly (especially outside of winter), more contemporary studies of gardening among Japanese Americans in Hawaii would suggest that many did. In the 1990s, Toshihiko Ikagawa's (1994, 84) survey of 100 households in Honolulu revealed that 97 percent of the families of Japanese origin took care of their own front yards rather than hiring someone else. Of these households, 73 percent reported that they worked in their yards on a daily, bi-weekly, or weekly basis—a rate at least 25 percent higher than that reported by families of all other ethnic backgrounds, who were more likely to engage in yard work only monthly. As Japanese garden expert Teiji Itoh (1973) notes, gardens are living things, and they require constant care. The physicality of that constant care brings health benefits to gardeners, benefits that extend from the health of the body to the health of the mind.

The Mind in the Garden

Researchers and practitioners have long noted the positive effect gardens can have in calming the mind. This is linked in general to societal beliefs that nature is a powerful force for well-being (Warner 1994, 5), a common attitude among those of Japanese ancestry. Shoji Nagumo, considered the father of Southern California gardeners (Hirahara 2000), promoted the profession, proclaiming that "gardening is healthy because it is done in nature" (cited in Seki 2007, 7). Other vocal proponents of both the physical and mental power of gardens come from the field of horticultural therapy. Their body of applied research has shown repeatedly the physio-psychological benefits of gardens and gardening, especially among stressed populations, be they in hospitals, rehabilitation facilities, or prisons (Ulrich 1999). Indeed, the research done at the last of these, sites of incarceration, helps us most understand Amache and the other WRA camps. My thinking about this owes a great deal to James Jiler's book *Doing Time in the Garden: Life Lessons through Prison Horticulture* (2006).

One of the most important psychological effects of gardening is the reduction of stress. In a survey of members of the American Horticultural Society, over 60 percent noted that even more than aesthetic or dietary benefits, gardens contributed to feelings of peacefulness and tranquility (Lewis 1994, 15). Likewise, studies of prison gardens point to three primary benefits: the quieting of mind, the reduction of stress, and a general sense of well-being (Jiler 2006). In particular, gardening gives people coping with depression, anger, and trauma an avenue to channel those feelings in a productive manner. In that way, gardens contribute to emotional recovery (Jiler 2006, 34).

Just how is it that gardens work their magic on the incarcerated? Several interrelated factors seem to be key, factors that likely also held true at Amache. As noted by Paula Hayes, a landscape designer who worked at Rikers Island, prisons are "relentlessly exposed landscapes" where "nothing is decorated or celebrated" (cited in Jiler 2006, 89), a destabilizing erasure of place. For prisoners, gardens become an oasis where personal space and a sense of the domestic (as opposed to the institutional) can be nurtured and cultivated. Jane E. Dusselier makes a similar claim for gardens at Japanese American confinement sites. They are a form of "re-territorialization," a location where people alter hostile landscapes into arenas in which individual identities can be expressed and group identity reaffirmed (Dusselier 2008).

The connection of Japanese identity to gardening comes through in my conversations with Amache survivors and their descendants. A daughter of Amache incarcerees made this comment about the gardens during her visit to the site: "We're Japanese. We grow things. It's what we do." Poet Sankyaku Seki (2007, 38), an American immigrant from Japan, suggests that gardening is part of "Nikkei consciousness." For people who had been displaced multiple times (from home to assembly center to a WRA camp), the act of literally putting down roots provided psychological stability of a form distinctly tied to an ancestral sense of self.

Something else gardens do for the incarcerated is create a more healthy relationship with time, a factor even more acute for those imprisoned at Amache who had no idea when (or even if) they would be returning home. As the director of the New York prison garden program puts it, "Time is not your friend in prison. It goes slow but not in the garden" (cited in Jiler 2006, 49). The connection to time comes in part through the meditative routine of garden work. But it also has to do with the cycle of plant growth, a cycle tied to daylight and seasons. Gardening ties life to a reassuring calendar: you plan, you plant, you nurture, you harvest. Even winter can be beautiful, especially in Japanese gardens, which are often designed with features for each season (figure 8.3). Gardening is also a productive use of time that otherwise can feel wasted; there's a reason incarceration is often called "doing time." If some of that time is spent gardening, prisoners can create something of which they can be proud, in part because it benefits the entire community.

This aspect—positive and visible change that is experienced not just by gardeners but by all who interact with gardens—is critical to their therapeutic success. As a commissioner of corrections notes, in prison gardens, people, not just plants, are grown (cited in Jiler 2006, 10). In prisons where composting is part of the program, the activity is a powerful metaphor; life's

FIGURE 8.3. 6H garden under the snow. *Courtesy*, Japanese American National Museum, Los Angeles (gift of Jack Muro, 2012.2.705).

mistakes and misfortunes can be transformed into something positive (36). These findings shine an interesting light on the archaeology at Amache, with its consistent evidence of composting and reuse of discarded materials. This metaphor for the value and transformative power in what some consider waste was probably not lost on incarcerees.

As suggested earlier, work in gardens can be a meditative practice, a benefit particularly valuable for the incarcerated. Prison inmates cited in Jiler (2006) repeatedly identified positive mental effects connected to the physical labor of gardening. For example, one inmate noted that gardening was the only activity in prison that cleared her mind and let her evaluate her life (149). Another inmate stated that gardens were soothing and kept worries at bay: "Gotta stay busy. Otherwise you think too much" (42).

One imagines that gardening was perhaps an even more powerful meditative practice for people of Japanese ancestry. The Issei in particular were raised in a culture shaped by centuries of religious and philosophical traditions emphasizing harmony not just in the final product of art but in its making. David A. Slawson, who apprenticed with master gardeners in Kyoto, writes of ways that approach can apply to gardening. After a long day of work, Slawson shifted to standing with all his weight on one foot, an act for which he was chided by his supervisor. The imbalance in his stance introduced a disturbance in the harmony of the garden. Slawson (1987, 13) notes that the lesson he learned was that the spirit with which one performs a task in a Japanese garden is even more important than getting the task done.

The chores of weeding, raking gravel, and cleaning up fallen leaves are acts Amacheans would have needed to perform to keep their gardens in balance. Although we have not found artifacts at Amache for raking gravel, historical accounts attest to the practice in other camps. At Amache we certainly have recovered other tools needed for the care of gardens: barrel hoops from the barrels that stored water, watering cans made from tin cans, and a homemade wheelbarrow wheel (see figure 7.11). Likewise, the recovery of pollen from plants difficult to grow on the High Plains, such as *Canna* and cattail, attests to the success of constant garden care.

Meeting Spiritual Needs

The history of Japanese gardens suggests that one should not overlook the role these places could have played in the spiritual life of incarcerees. Indeed, the needs for beauty, a connection to nature, and balance come together in gardens.

Beauty and spirit can be deeply entwined, as evidenced in the strong tradition of religious art in Japan—from statuary to poetry to gardens. Many of the most important designers of gardens in medieval Japan were Buddhist monks, the most famous of whom were associated with the *karesansui*—dry landscape gardens—of Zen temples. They were preceded by the "stone-setting priests" of the Shingon sect of Buddhism, whose founder believed art was the path to enlightenment. The stone-setting priests filled their gardens with stones and also trees and ponds that evoked sacred Buddhist cosmology.

Yet art does not need to be religious to be spiritual, especially for many Japanese. Based in part on his conversations with incarcerees both during and after the war, Allen H. Eaton (1952, 116) claimed that for those he spoke to, "the innate recognition of the fitting thing, the beautiful thing—even in the simplest circumstances of life—is a basic principle; it is in reality a religion." In a place of upheaval like the camps, art served as a powerful avenue to internal peace. It is the sort of situation like the war-torn areas writer Terry Tempest Williams reflects upon where "art is not optional, but a strategy for survival" (quoted in Rheannon 2008).

A good example of garden art at Amache is the park next to the town hall discussed in chapter 6. Built as a community endeavor, it was carefully designed with considerable effort. Someone even managed to catch live fish from the Arkansas River to fulfill the role of more traditional *koi*. As captured in posed portraits and snapshots, this was a place of beauty where Amacheans could be rightfully proud of the community they had worked so hard to make.

But it wasn't just the public gardens that were bright spots in camp; even the vegetable gardens were aesthetically pleasing. The series of family photos of the Hiranos in their vegetable entryway garden (see figure 6.1) indicates their pride in its appearance. Excavations in which we recovered *Canna* from a victory garden suggest that the Hiranos weren't alone in wanting even a vegetable garden to be beautiful. Not only does *Canna* have a colorful bloom, its shiny black seeds could be used artistically. Likewise, the gourds grown in camp gardens were sometimes crafted into art pieces (see figure 1.3). Gardens were not only pleasing locales, they provided materials for other types of aesthetic expression.

At Amache and the other WRA camps, making art was driven in part by moral imperative. If you had an artistic skill, you should share it with your community (Dusselier 2008). We see this expressed in the hundreds of art classes taught by incarcerees in all the camps. Like other traditional Japanese art forms, many gardeners could have learned from the experts in camp who had more training or experience. In her thesis research on gardens at Manzanar, Laura Ng (2014) noted that many who gardened there were not professionally trained, a finding that aligns with Amache. Training at Amache would have happened more formally through organizations like the "garden club," for which secondary school students could receive credit. Group gardening projects like the town hall park and the landscaping of the elementary school would have provided other opportunities for Amacheans across camp to learn techniques from one another. In fact, calls for assistance with such landscaping projects were published in both the English- and Japanese-language sections of the Amache newspaper. Most collaborations and thus opportunities for learning would likely have happened at a smaller scale—within a block or between nearby neighbors. That kind of sharing of ideas and techniques probably contributed to the distinctive landscape patterns we see in some of Amache's barracks blocks (Kamp-Whittaker and Clark 2019).

Involving the children of the camps in art had a particularly strong imperative, driven in part by concern that they would grow up aesthetically stunted by the ugliness of their surroundings (Helphand 2006). Shoji Nagumo's biography, which reflects back on his experience at Heart Mountain, strongly states this worry: "When I thought about children being raised in the desert without grass or trees, I was sure they would become human beings who would not feel joy or pleasure in anything. They might even grow up not understanding the beauty of Nature" (cited in Hirahara 2000, 53). This, he stated, was the impetus behind his work planting trees and victory gardens at Heart Mountain, a sentiment likely shared by incarerees in all the camps.

Gardens in Japan are considered a gift not only to one's family but to all who see them (Itoh 1973, 88). At Amache, gardens were a particularly impactful source of beauty for the community. My conversations with Helen Yagi Sekikawa suggest that her grandfather's garden was crafted not just for the enjoyment of his extended family, who were often photographed there (figure 8.4). The spectacular Umeda garden wrapped in a U shape around the barrack next to one of the two Buddhist temples at Amache. Many of the congregants would have walked past that garden on their way to temple. Helen (2013) noted that as a Buddhist himself, her grandfather's garden was likely seen as an act of devotion—something to share with those on their way to worship.

Beauty as a gift to the community is echoed in the poetry of Lawson Fusao Inada. His "Children of the Camps" contains these lines: "The people made poetry / with their very own hands   / little gifts of scrap / for precious loved ones, / Friends, elders, children" (Inada 1997, 116).

A connection to nature was a spiritual need that was likely felt by many at Amache and was one uniquely met by its gardens. The importance of that connection is woven throughout Japanese belief and culture, whether it is the fine tradition of landscape art, moon viewing, nature poetry, or yearly festivals such as *sakura matsuri*, when communities celebrate the blossoming cherry trees. It is one of the foundational principles of Japanese gardening. As designer Hoichi Kurisu (2016, 6) writes, "The time-honored techniques of Japanese garden design were developed to direct one's experience in specific

FIGURE 8.4. Matiji Umeda's daughter and granddaughter photographed in his garden. *Courtesy*, Helen Yagi Sekikawa.

ways, to lessen preoccupation with the self and foster an increased awareness of nature and our relation to it." Shinto is often identified as the foundation for this connection, for the source of power in Shinto is nature itself. It is there—in mountains or bodies of water or individual rocks or trees—that we find *kami*, the spirit of the divine. The *kami* in stone helps explain its primacy in Japanese garden design. The earliest Japanese gardening guides devote much of their text to the proper ways of setting stones. They also make it clear that a belief in *kami* coexisted with Buddhist and Daoist thought. Modern gardening books suggest that these beliefs are still strong in Japan today. Likewise, ethnographic work with people of Japanese descent in both the United States and Brazil indicates that a belief in *kami* is sustained even by converts to Christianity (Nakamaki 2003, 134).

Despite the local geology of stabilized sand dunes, archaeology indicates that stone remained a key element in the gardens of the camp. The most important source for this material was probably the Arkansas River, with beaches and sand bars containing rocks ranging from gravel to large river cobble. Unlike the builders of the town hall garden, most incarceree gardeners would have had to haul such materials back without the use of camp vehicles, yet such efforts appear to have been commonplace. Limestone exposed in the root cellars and other subterranean camp facilities was another source for stone. Limestone tended to be used in gardens in common areas, like those at the elementary school. Crushed, it was used to surface the camp's main roads and sidewalks, and it may be that quarrying limestone was sanctioned by camp officials. Finally, many in Amache appear to have kept an eye open for interesting stone on their excursions away from camp, and the entryway gardens attest to their success. One of the most intriguing of such stones is a piece of magnetite, which crews recovered during excavations of the Okumuras' *karesansui* garden. As a rock that is actually magnetic, this is one stone whose *kami* could have been particularly acute.

It was not only in seeking stone that incarcerees turned to the gifts of nature. At Amache and other camps, incarceree gardeners were returning to the roots of Japanese gardening—where nature was the nursery (Helphand 2006, 168). Several of the blocks we have surveyed appear to have had public-area gardens composed primarily of river gravel and prickly pear cactus. Such cactus gardens have been recorded at other WRA camps as well (Helphand 2006). In addition to cactus, archaeology reveals other wild transplants at Amache, including plants from the Arkansas River, and humble ground cover like purslane, which we recovered in high numbers from several of the excavated gardens.

Gardens in Japan connect people to nature in many ways, including sharpening awareness of the changing of the seasons. Ideally, a Japanese-style garden includes elements that are at their peak of interest throughout every season (for example, grasses are associated with fall because they capture the wind, while evergreens maintain color throughout the winter). An appreciation for the seasons is reflected in the poetry written by Nikkei professional gardeners in the United States: "The power of spring is seen as the weeds grow where they were thrown away" (Seki 2007, 11).

One of the more surprising insights from our pollen analysis is how common flowering shrubs and trees were in Amache's gardens. We have recovered pollen from both dogwood and the *Prunus* family, which includes plums and cherries. These were likely procured from a nursery at some expense. In a place where the future was very uncertain, their spring flowering would have marked time in a reassuring and sensorially pleasing way. They shared with all the deciduous trees a natural foliage clock: first leafing out, then greening up, changing color, and finally falling. Likewise, the water features at camp would have frozen and thawed with the seasons. Their surfaces would have reflected the changing conditions of the sky, another familiar seasonal touchstone.

Providing an avenue for harmony and balance may have been the most important way these gardens met spiritual needs. The incarcerees lived in a world where the social ground was constantly shifting. One day they were farmers or optometrists, the next they were prisoners with no idea when or if they might be released. The Issei were people without a country, while their Nisei children were citizens of a country that had turned its back on them. But they had a skill set honed over generations for bringing harmony to at least one little part of the world—their garden.

In this assertion, I am inspired by several of my former students whose thesis research takes issue with theories of power and control used in many incarceration camp studies (Driver 2015; Garrison 2015). A primary model (Foucault 1979) suggests that when a powerful agent asserts dominance, those under its control will react with resistance (see Casella 2007 for an overview of its application to the archaeology of institutional confinement). Kenneth I. Helphand (2006, 189), a scholar of gardens in many prison-like settings, reflects this idea when he writes of WRA camp gardens, "All of these gardens, grand and small, were acts of resistance." Others suggest that in gardens, incarcerees could assert control in a situation in which they were often powerless (e.g., Tamura 2004, 13).

The more I have come to know these gardens, the people who made them, and the history of Japanese gardens, the more I have also come to question these models. The deep literature on Japanese gardening past and present never dwells on control; in fact, it often reminds practitioners that a garden will always be beyond their control. This comes through in acknowledging that stones have a will of their own and assertions that plants have their own nature against which gardeners should never force them (e.g., Itoh 1973, 88–89). Indeed, only in respecting the power of nature can one come to peace, which, as some claim, is the ultimate goal of a Japanese garden (e.g., Kawana 1977).

Rather than a focus on dominion (over space, over nature), a more appropriate emphasis for these confinement site gardens is the search for balance and harmony. As noted earlier, one avenue for achieving balance is through the physical practice of gardening. Another is in the careful aesthetic balance of garden design. As one scholar noted, a proper Japanese garden "must have a balanced sense of both flow and calm" (Hayakawa 1973, 134). This can be achieved in numerous ways, each supported by tradition. For example, one can mimic nature, with overlapping plantings and asymmetrical design. The 11H, Barrack 9 garden achieves this in a seamless connection of inside and outside space. Another tactic is to distill nature to its most basic forms. Such gardens are meant to impart internal balance to those who meditate on them. The seascape of the Okumura garden does this despite limited access to the large stones of more typical *karesansui* gardens.

Another element of harmony created by the Amache gardeners is a kind of deep balance, which we discovered through our study of soil chemistry. In the majority of garden features we have tested, the soil retains a higher nutrient and organic carbon content than that of control pits dug both within the site in non-garden areas and outside the site (figure 8.5). Considering the site's porous sandy matrix and the short duration of the camp's occupation, this imprint is nothing short of amazing. There remains, seventy-five years later, a legacy of care for this land by a people who were forced to inhabit it.

Conclusion

Although to this point the physical, psychological, and spiritual benefits of gardening have been discussed separately, to really grapple with the Amache gardens or any garden, one must think holistically. Muso Soseki, often credited with creating the first Zen temple gardens, wrote, "He who distinguishes between the garden and practice cannot be said to have found the true Way" (cited in Berthier 2005, 3). Indeed, physical labor in gardens is for many living Nikkei an act of devotion, an idea elegantly expressed in a postwar gardener's poem: "In the next world, I want to sweep the fallen leaves in God's Garden" (Seki 2007, 33).

As incarcerees created and maintained their gardens, they were expressing hope not just for the world but for themselves as a part of it. To quote Japanese gardening expert Teiji Itoh (1973, 89), "If a man respects himself, then he must

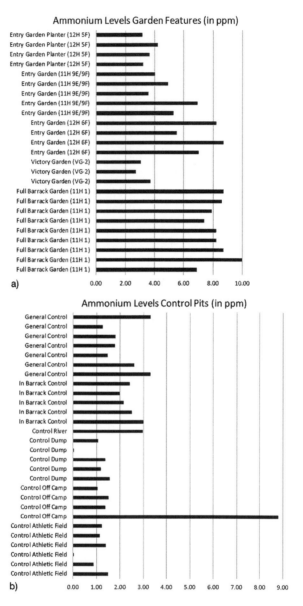

FIGURE 8.5. With a few exceptions, soils in garden strata (a) tend to contain much higher levels of useful nutrients than soil in control plots (b). A good example is ammonium (NH4), an important soil nutrient and often a component of commercial fertilizer that is charted here in parts per million (ppm). *Courtesy*, Courtney Seffense.

also respect the trees and stones that nature has created. It was nature itself, maintaining harmony among the countless elements of its own creation, that served as the supreme model for the garden." Ultimately, in the way it fused art and act, place and spirit, mind and body, gardening was a material practice especially suited to help the people of Japanese ancestry imprisoned at Amache cope with a nearly unlivable situation.

Epilogue

Gardens and Giri

In my old age I still have a lot of dreams which will remain
in the soil I fought for.

Poem by a Nikkei gardener, in Seki 2007, 37

During field school orientation, I introduce my students to the Japanese philosophy of *giri*. It involves a set of obligations to take care of others, to follow
the "righteous way" (Seki 1971, 106). Within families, it may mean putting
another's needs before one's own. In informal relationships, *giri* can take the
form of small gifts, tokens of thoughtfulness for the other that bind the community. But importantly, *giri* does not come in the form of an explicit request.
It is an often unspoken sense of obligation and care, one that has been explic-
itly applied to Nikkei heritage (Kishaba 2003).

The physical remains at Amache exist in the world of *giri*; they are both a
gift and an obligation. Framing their engagement with the site in the web of
giri helps my students translate the ethical codes of archaeology (such as site
stewardship) into terms the incarcerees at Amache would have understood.

DOI: 10.5876/9781646420933.c009

It also, importantly, highlights that our work brings us into a relationship, both with those who left behind these physical items and with those who might encounter them in the future. If we treat this site with *giri*, it will last for generations to come.

Can a site of institutional confinement really be a gift? One could expect it to be negative heritage, "a repository of negative memory in the collective imaginary" (Meskell 2002, 558). And certainly, the evidence uncovered during this research speaks to physical, economic, and psychological stresses. But our work, especially in the gardens, also tells a different story, one where hope was literally planted into the soil—hope for a seed to sprout, a tree to shade, a flower to bloom. Gardens were a gift from the incarcerees to themselves and to each other. They were also, it turns out, a gift to the future. The gardens of Amache are repositories of generational knowledge. In them, a philosophical stance toward nature is made manifest through horticultural skill. They reveal a hybrid aesthetic with deep roots in the homeland but informed by the front yards of America. Materials employed in the gardens evidence incarceree networks and ingenuity. In these gardens an uprooted people reclaimed a connection to the land, often through discovery of local resources, like drought-resistant plants or river cobbles worn smooth by their journey from the mountains.

Reclaiming connections continues today, as former incarcerees and their families return to Amache. At the site they walk with their ancestors, sometimes armed like detectives with a few clues—a family photograph, a story told in passing. If it is a windy day (which it usually is), they literally get a taste of the place. A drink of cold water will wash the grit out of their mouths, but its taste lingers and informs. At our garden excavation sites, visitors see how incarcerees combated that dust, not just with curses but also with beauty. Here they learn a different story as read through the land and have one more reason to be proud of their ancestors' legacy. As one of my volunteers wrote in his personal field journal, "By being at the site, I have gained a greater respect for my parents' determination to make the best of a bad situation: to endure with perseverance and dignity, and to thrive."

By combining intensive landscape archaeology with community engagement, work at Amache is enabling the site to come alive. My crews and I reveal a past community and the strategies of the individuals within it. By working and talking together, we are also part of a new community centered around both the tangible and intangible heritage of this site. Despite our varied backgrounds, we all share a physical experience of this place that for so long was in the shadows. We also share a commitment to preserving this critical locale not just because it is a significant historical resource, which it is, but because we owe it to those who so carefully remade it.

It is not just through archaeology that the gardens at Amache live on. When the camp was closed in 1945, residents of the town of Granada gathered materials from the camp gardens. A stand of lilacs still growing in an alleyway near the Amache Museum was transplanted from the camp. By insisting on a livable environment, Amacheans ended up improving that of their neighbors as well. As in the jar of seeds with which this book began, it is likely that some of the genetic material of the Amache gardens lives on elsewhere. Kei and Yamato Ichihashi left Amache in the spring of 1945 for their home in Stanford, California. They were delighted when friends sent them morning glory seeds from the camp. Within only a few days, the flowers took hold in their home garden (Chang 1997, 449). Back at Amache, it is not just the Siberian elms that bear witness to the camp's landscape; even today, a few roses grow in front of one barrack foundation. These roses are a hardy variety, and like the people who put them there, they bring beauty and life to the harsh land in which they were planted.

Appendix
Taxa List of Likely Garden Plants at Amache

Common Name	Taxa	Data Source
Introduced Plants		
blackberry	*Rubus*	pollen
canna lily	*Canna*	pollen / phytolith
clover	*Trifolium*	pollen
cockscomb / amaranth	*Alternanthera*	pollen
dogwood	*Cornus*	pollen
elderberry	*Sambucus*	pollen
evening primrose family	Onagraceae	pollen
hackberry	*Celtis*	pollen
lily	Liliaceae	pollen
mallow	Malvaceae	pollen
mint family	Lamiaceae	pollen
morning glory	*Ipomoea*	flotation / documents
narrow leaf cattail	*Typha angustifolia*	pollen

DOI: 10.5876/9781646420933.c010

Continued

Common Name	Taxa	Data Source
parsley family	Apiaceae	pollen
petunia	*Petunia*	flotation
pine	*Pinus*	pollen / flotation
plum / cherry family	*Prunus*	pollen
potato	*Solanum tuberosum*	pollen
rose	Rosaceae	pollen / current plants (Rugosa variety currently present on site)
rye and other cooler climate grasses	Festucoid	pollen / documents / oral history
Siberian elm	*Ulmus pumila*	flotation / pollen / oral history / current plants
squash / gourd / melon	*Curcurbitaceae*	flotation / documents / oral history
sumac	*Rhus*	pollen

Plants with Both Introduced and Native Varieties

mustard family	Brassicacae	pollen / flotation
phlox	Polemoniaceae	pollen
prairie coneflower	*Dalea (Petalostemum)*	pollen
purslane	*Portulaca*	flotation
verbena / vervain	*Verbena*	flotation

Native Plants

bush morning glory	*Ipomoea leptophylla*	documents
caltrop	*Kallstroemia*	flotation
cholla	*Cylindropuntia imbricata*	current plant
cottonwood	*Populus deltoides*	documents
goldenrod group	Asteraceae (Low Spine)	flotation / pollen
pepperweed	*Lepidium*	flotation
prairie sunflower	*Helianthus petiolaris*	flotation
prickly pear cactus	*Opuntia*	flotation / pollen / documents
prickly poppy	*Argemone*	flotation
redwhisker clammyweed	*Polanisia dodecandra*	flotation
sunflower group	Asteraceae (High Spine)	flotation / pollen

Glossary

archaeobotany. The study of plant remains recovered from archaeological deposits.

CWRIC. The Commission on Wartime Relocation and Internment of Civilians was summoned by the US Congress to study all federal government documents related to Japanese Americans in World War II. Its findings contributed to federal legislation that provided reparations for Japanese Americans incarcerated during the war.

exclusion zone. An area of the United States from which individuals can be excluded based on criteria related to national security. Exclusion zones were made possible by the signing of Executive Order 9066.

flotation. Technique to separate macrobotanical remains from soil using water to make plant remains float.

giri. Literally "the righteous way," it is a Japanese practice of reciprocity with overtones of both gift and obligation.

GPR. Ground-penetrating radar is an instrument that uses energy pulses to produce three-dimensional maps of buried materials.

DOI: 10.5876/9781646420933.c011

High Plains. A semiarid, windy region of the United States located between the Rocky Mountains and the Great Plains.

in situ. Latin term used for items found in place during archaeological excavations.

Issei. Term used for first-generation Japanese immigrants, derived from the Japanese word for "first."

kami. A Shinto-based belief in the divine spirit within all things, especially those found in nature.

karesansui. A Japanese garden style traditionally composed primarily of gravel and rock with isolated plantings. *Karesansui* means "dry mountain water" in Japanese.

Kibei. Nisei who were educated in Japan.

macrobotanical remains. Plant remans that can be seen with the naked eye, such a seeds, bark, and roots.

Meiji era. Time period (AD 1868–1912) when Japan returned to Imperial rule and opened up to Westernization. The majority of Japanese immigration to the United States occurred during the Meiji era.

microbotanical remains. Plant remains that must be identified using a microscope, such as pollen and phytoliths.

MP. Military Police. At Amache, they guarded the front gate and manned the guard towers.

Nikkei. People of Japanese ancestry living outside Japan.

Nisei. Term used for the children of Japanese immigrants, derived from the Japanese word for "second." If born in the United States, Nisei were automatically citizens.

niwa. The primary Japanese word for garden.

palynology. The study of pollen.

phytoliths. Silica bodies produced by many types of plants to give them stability.

roji. A meandering path in a Japanese-style garden meant to invoke walking through the forest.

Seinan. A neighborhood in southwest Los Angeles that was the pre-war home of many individuals incarcerated at Amache. The name derives from the Japanese word for "southwest."

Shinto. A Japanese religion that grew out of a set of folk beliefs about the power of nature.

tsuboniwa. Gardens found in courtyards or other small spaces in Japan. The term combines the word for garden (*niwa*) with that of a unit of measurement (the *tsubo*, which covers an area about 10 square feet, or 3.3 m^2).

WRA. War Relocation Authority. A civilian agency of the federal government charged with the removal, confinement, and relocation of Japanese Americans during World War II.

Yamato Colonies. Three farming colonies located in the Central Valley of California whose entire populations were removed to Amache. The Yamato Colonies—now better known as Livingston, Cortez, and Cressey—were founded by prominent businessman Kyutaro Abiko.

References

Adachi, Nobuko, ed. 2006. *Japanese Diasporas: Unsung Pasts, Conflicting Presents, and Uncertain Futures*. London: Routledge.

Ancestry.com. 2011. "City Directory, Los Angeles."

Aoki, Kazie Yoshida. 1998. Amache Relocation Camp Reunion '98 Commemorative Calendar (annotated). Amache Historical Society, Granada, CO.

Archer, Steven N. 2009. *Amache Garden Testing 2008—Archaeobotanical Analysis*. University of Denver, Department of Anthropology, DU Amache Project Files.

Archer, Steven N. 2012. "Amache Garden Testing—2010 Field Season Archaeobotanical Analysis." In *Archaeological Investigations at the Granada Relocation Center (Amache), National Historic Landmark, Prowers County, Colorado: Report on the 2010 Field Season*, by Bonnie J. Clark, David Garrison, and Paul Swader, appendix A. Prepared for History Colorado, State Historical Fund. University of Denver, Department of Anthropology.

Archer, Steven N. 2015. "Amache Test Excavations—2012 Field Season Archaeobotanical Analysis." In *Archaeological Investigations at the Granada Relocation Center (Amache), National Historic Landmark, Prowers County, Colorado: Report on the 2012 Field Season*, by Christian Driver and Bonnie J. Clark, appendix B. Prepared for History Colorado, State Historical Fund. University of Denver, Department of Anthropology.

DOI: 10.5876/9781646420933.c012

Archer, Steven N., with contributions by Martha McCartney, Lucie Vinciguerra, Andrew Edwards, and Edward Chappell. 2015. *Archaeology of the Wren Garden.* Colonial Williamsburg Foundation Library Research Report Series. Williamsburg, VA: Colonial Williamsburg Foundation Library. https://research.colonial williamsburg.org/DigitalLibrary/view/index.cfm?doc=ResearchReports \RR1760.xml&highlight=wren%20garden.

Asakawa, Gil. 2012. *Granada Pioneer* (newspaper). In *Densho Encyclopedia*, edited by Brian Niya. http://encyclopedia.densho.org/Granada_Pioneer_(newspaper)/.

Basso, Keith. 1996. *Wisdom Sits in Places: Landscape and Language among the Western Apache.* Albuquerque: University of New Mexico Press.

Bender, Barbara. 2002. "Time and Landscape." *Current Anthropologist* 43 (S4): S103–S112.

Berthier, François. 2005. *Reading Zen in the Rocks: The Japanese Dry Landscape Garden.* Edited by Graham Parkes. Chicago: University of Chicago Press.

Brown, Kendall H. 1999. "Territories of Play: A Short History of Japanese-Style Gardens in North America." In *Japanese-Style Gardens of the Pacific West Coast*, edited by Kendall H. Brown, 8–29. New York: Rizzoli.

Brown, Kendall H. 2013. *Quiet Beauty: The Japanese Gardens of North America.* Tokyo: Tuttle.

Burton, Jeffery F. 2015. *Garden Management Plan: Gardens and Gardeners at Manzanar.* Manzanar National Historic Site, CA: National Park Service, US Department of the Interior. https://www.nps.gov/manz/learn/management/upload/Man zanar-Garden-Management-Plan-2015.pdf.

Burton, Jeffery F., Mary M. Farrell, Florence B. Lord, and Richard W. Lord. 2002. *Confinement and Ethnicity: An Overview of World War II Japanese American Relocation Sites.* Seattle: University of Washington Press.

Butler, Kim D. 2001. "Defining Diaspora, Refining a Discourse." *Diaspora: A Journal of Transnational Studies* 10 (2): 180–219.

Carrillo, Richard F., and David Killam. 2004. "Camp Amache (5PW48): A Class III Intensive Field Survey of the Granada Relocation Center, Prowers County, Colorado." Prepared by RMC Consultants, Inc., for the Town of Granada.

Casella, Eleanor Conlin. 2007. *The Archaeology of Institutional Confinement: The American Experience in Archaeological Perspective.* Gainesville: University Press of Florida.

Casey, Lee. 1942. "The Strangest City in Colorado." *Rocky Mountain News*, November 25.

Castañeda, Quetzil E., and Christopher Matthews, eds. 2008. *Ethnographic Archaeologies: Reflections on Stakeholders and Archaeological Practices.* Lanham, MD: Altamira.

Chang, Gordon H., ed. 1997. *Morning Glory, Evening Shadow: Yamato Ichihashi and His Internment Writings, 1942–1945.* Stanford, CA: Stanford University Press.

Chiang, Connie Y. 2010. "Imprisoned Nature: Toward an Environmental History of the World War II Japanese American Incarceration." *Environmental History* 15: 236–267.

Clark, Bonnie J. 2011. *On the Edge of Purgatory: An Archaeology of Place in Hispanic Colorado*. Historical Archaeology of the American West. Series editors Annalies Corbin and Rebecca Allen. Lincoln: University of Nebraska Press and the Society for Historical Archaeology.

Clark, Bonnie J. 2016. "Are Trump Supporters Seriously Citing the Internment of Japanese Americans as a Model?" *History News Network*. November 18. http:// https://historynewsnetwork.org/article/164447.

Clark, Bonnie J., David Garrison, and Paul Swader. 2012. *Archaeological Investigations at the Granada Relocation Center (Amache), National Historic Landmark, Prowers County, Colorado: Report on the 2010 Field Season*. Prepared for History Colorado, State Historical Fund. University of Denver, Department of Anthropology.

Clark, Bonnie J., April Kamp-Whittaker, and Dana Ogo Shew. 2008. *The Tangible History of Amache: Research Design and Methodology for Field Investigations, Summer 2008*. University of Denver, Department of Anthropology.

Clark, Bonnie J., and Laura L. Scheiber. 2008. "A Sloping Land: An Introduction to Archaeological Landscapes on the High Plains." In *Archaeological Landscapes on the High Plains*, edited by Laura L. Scheiber and Bonnie J. Clark, 1–16. Boulder: University Press of Colorado.

Colorado Preservation, Inc. 2010. *Dismantling Amache: Building Stock Research and Inventory Related to the Granada Relocation Center*. Denver: Report prepared for Friends of Amache.

Conyers, Lawrence. 2012. *Interpreting Ground-Penetrating Radar for Archaeology*. Walnut Creek, CA: Left Coast.

Conyers, Lawrence. 2013. *Ground-Penetrating Radar for Archaeology*, 3rd ed. Latham, MD: Rowman and Littlefield and Altamira.

Currie, Christopher. 2005. *Garden Archaeology: A Handbook*. York: Council for British Archaeology.

Curtis, Henry S. 1927. "The Grounds of the Elementary School." *Journal of Education* 105 (18): 472.

CWRIC, Commission on Wartime Relocation and Internment of Civilians. 1992. *Personal Justice Denied: Report of the Commission on Wartime Relocation and Internment of Civilians*. Seattle: University of Washington Press.

Daniels, Roger. 1972. *Concentration Camps USA: Japanese Americans and World War II*. New York: Holt, Rinehart, and Winston.

Daniels, Roger. 1986. "The Forced Migration of West Coast Japanese Americans, 1941–1946: A Quantitative Note." In *Japanese Americans: From Relocation to Redress*, edited by Roger Daniels, Sandra C. Taylor, and Harry H.L. Kitano, 72–74. Salt Lake City: University of Utah Press.

Daniels, Roger. 1993. *Prisoners without Trial: Japanese Americans in World War II*. Edited by Eric Foner. Critical Issues (series). New York: Hill and Wang.

Daniels, Roger. 2008. "Words Do Matter: A Note on Inappropriate Terminology and the Incarceration of the Japanese Americans." *Discover Nikkei*. http://www .discovernikkei.org/en/journal/2008/2/6/words-do-matter/.

Deetz, James. 1996. *In Small Things Forgotten*. Expanded and revised ed. New York: Anchor Books.

Denoon, Donald, and Gavan McCormack, eds. 1996. *Multicultural Japan: Palaeolithic to Postmodern*. Cambridge, NY: Cambridge University Press.

DeWitt, J. L. 1943. *Final Report: Japanese Evacuation from the West Coast*. Washington, DC: Government Printing Office.

Domoto, Kaneji, and George Kay. 1974. *Bonsai and the Japanese Garden: Applying the Ancient Bonsai Art and Japanese Landscaping to America's Gardens*. Barrington, IL: A. B. Morse, Countryside Books.

Dowling, Sarah. 2014. "'How Lucky I Was to Be Free and Safe at Home': Reading Humor in Miné Okubo's Citizen 13660." *Signs* 39 (2): 299–322.

Driver, Christian. 2015. "Brewing behind Barbed Wire: An Archaeology of Saké at Amache." MA thesis, Department of Anthropology, University of Denver.

Driver, Christian, and Bonnie J. Clark. 2015. *Archaeological Investigations at the Granada Relocation Center (Amache), National Historic Landmark, Prowers County, Colorado: Report on the 2012 Field Season*. Prepared for History Colorado, State Historical Fund. University of Denver, Department of Anthropology.

DU Amache. 2009. Notes from the 2009 Amache Reunion. University of Denver, Department of Anthropology, DU Amache Project Files.

DU Amache. 2011. Notes from an Amache Community Meeting. University of Denver, Department of Anthropology, DU Amache Project Files.

Dumas, Enoch, and Margaret Walther. 1944. "Landscaping for Beauty and Health." *School Executive* (May): 40–41.

Dusselier, Jane E. 2008. *Artifacts of Loss: Crafting Survival in Japanese American Concentration Camps*. New Brunswick, NJ: Rutgers University Press.

Eaton, Allen H. 1952. *Beauty behind Barbed Wire: The Arts of the Japanese in Our War Relocation Camps*. New York: Harper.

Eggleston, Emily C. 2012. "How Japanese American Gardeners Shaped an Internment Camp Landscape: Soil Chemistry and Archival Analysis." MS thesis, Department of Geography, University of Wisconsin–Madison.

Eliovson, Sima. 1970. *Gardening the Japanese Way*. Wellington, New Zealand: A. H. and A. W. Reed.

Embree, John. 1943. "Report on Granada, January 30–February 1, 1943." In *Community Analysis Section, 1*, edited by War Relocation Authority. Berkeley: Bancroft Library, University of California.

Enmanji Buddhist Temple. 2016. "History of Enmanji." http://www.sonic.net /~enmanji/Enmanji/History.html.

Foucault, Michel. 1979. *Discipline and Punish: The Birth of the Prison.* Translated by Alan Sheridan. New York: Vintage Books.

Foxhoven, David. 1998. *Amache Reunion Interviews* (videorecording). Available at the Denver Public Library, Denver, CO.

Fujii, Eijirô. 2014. "Agricultural Landscapes as Seen in Edo-Period Gardens." Professional presentation, Tôyô Bunko, Japan, March 16.

Fujita, Dennis K. 2011. "The 1928 Fujita Property Case and California Alien Land Laws." Manuscript in possession of author.

Fukutake, Tadashi. 1980. *Rural Society in Japan.* Tokyo: University of Tokyo Press.

Garrison, David. 2015. "A History of Transplants: A Study of Entryway Gardens at Amache." MA thesis, Department of Anthropology, University of Denver.

Gebhard, Jessica Penelope Sewell. 2015. "Community Identity in the Granada Pioneer." MA thesis, Department of Anthropology, University of Denver.

Geertz, Clifford. 1996. "Afterword." In *Senses of Place,* edited by Steven Feld and Keith H. Basso, 259–262. Santa Fe, NM: School of American Research Press.

Geis, Shannon, and Rae Soloman. 2019. "Denver Orbit." In *Episode Thirty-Four: Nine Zero Six Six.* http://www.denverorbit.com/podcast/episode-thirty-four-nine-zero-six-six/.

Gesensway, Deborah, and Mindy Roseman. 1987. *Beyond Words: Images from America's Concentration Camps.* Ithaca, NY: Cornell University Press.

Gómez, Esteban M. 2016. "Trump and the Echo of Amache." *Sapiens: Anthropology/Everything Human* (November 7). https://www.sapiens.org/archaeology/children-of-amache/.

Granada Pioneer. 1943a. "Oriental Vegetable Seed Needed." *Granada Pioneer,* December 8, 9.

Granada Pioneer. 1943b. "A Success: 3000 Witness Flowers, Gardens." *Granada Pioneer,* November 17, 2.

Granada Pioneer. 1943c. "1,000 Bushels of Spinach Sent to Army, Poston, Gila." *Granada Pioneer,* June 12, 1.

Granada Pioneer. 1943d. "Thumbnail Sketches." *Granada Pioneer,* March 20, 6.

Granada Pioneer. 1943e. "Short Takes." *Granada Pioneer,* March 20, 2.

Granada Pioneer. 1943f. "Fair Draws 700 Outside Guests." *Granada Pioneer,* September 15, 1, 4.

Granada Pioneer. 1943g. "Agricultural Fair Winners." *Granada Pioneer,* September 15, 1, 4.

Granada Pioneer. 1943h. "Students Donate 'V' Garden Crops." *Granada Pioneer,* August 4, 6.

Granada Pioneer. 1944. "Need Volunteers for Landscaping." *Granada Pioneer,* April 15, 8, 10.

Haas, Jeremy, Zachary Starke, Bonnie J. Clark, and April Kamp-Whittaker. 2017. *Archaeological Investigations at the Granada Relocation Center (Amache), National Historic Landmark, Prowers County, Colorado: Report on the University of Denver 2014*

Field Season. Prepared for History Colorado, State Historical Fund. University of Denver, Department of Anthropology.

Harrison, Rodney, and John Schofield. 2010. *After Modernity: Archaeological Approaches to the Contemporary Past.* Oxford: Oxford University Press.

Harvey, Robert. 2003. *Amache: The Story of Japanese Internment in Colorado during World War II.* Dallas, TX: Taylor Trade Publishing, distributed by National Book Network.

Hashimoto, Takehiko. 1998. "The Introduction of the Metric System to Japan." In *The Introduction of Modern Science and Technology to Turkey and Japan,* edited by Feza Günergun and Shigehisa Kuriyama, 187–203. Kyoto: International Research Center for Japanese Studies.

Havens, Thomas R.H. 1974. *Farm and Nation in Modern Japan: Agrarian Nationalism, 1870–1940.* Princeton, NJ: Princeton University Press.

Havey, Lily Yuriko Nakai. 2014. *Gasa Gasa Girl Goes to Camp: A Nisei Youth behind a World War II Fence.* Edited by Cherstin M. Lyon. Salt Lake City: University of Utah Press.

Havey, Lily Yuriko Nakai. 2016. "Purple Cactus." http://www.lilyyurikohavey.com /gallery?lightbox=image_mir.

Hawley, Kevin. 2016. "Laboratory Report, Historical Archaeology." University of Denver, Department of Anthropology, DU Amache Project Files.

Hayakawa, Masao. 1973. *The Garden Art of Japan.* New York: Weatherhill.

Hayami, Yuhiro. 1964. "Demand for Fertilizer in the Course of Japanese Agricultural Development." *Journal of Farm Economics* 46: 766–779.

Hayashi, Brian Masaru. 2013. Informants / "inu." *Densho Encyclopedia.* https:// encyclopedia.densho.org/Informants%20/%20%22inu%22/.

Heimburger, Christian. 2008. *Life beyond Barbed Wire: Japanese American Labor during Internment at Amache and Topaz.* Thompson Writing Awards series, Center of the American West. Boulder: University of Colorado.

Heimburger, Christian. 2013. "Life beyond Barbed Wire: The Significance of Japanese American Labor in the Mountain West, 1942–1944." MA thesis, Department of History, University of Colorado at Boulder.

Helphand, Kenneth I. 2006. *Defiant Gardens: Making Gardens in Wartime.* San Antonio, TX: Trinity University Press.

Hirabayashi, Lane Ryo. 1999. *The Politics of Fieldwork: Research in an American Concentration Camp.* Tucson: University of Arizona Press.

Hirahara, Naomi, ed. 2000. *Greenmakers: Japanese American Gardeners in Southern California.* Los Angeles: Southern California Gardeners' Federation.

Hirano, George. 2011. Interview with DU Amache, edited by Bonnie J. Clark, Christian Driver, and David Garrison. Manuscript on file, Department of Anthropology, University of Denver.

Hirano, George. 2014. Interview with DU Amache, edited by Bonnie J. Clark and Zachary Starke. Manuscript on file, Department of Anthropology, University of Denver.

Hirano, Kiyo. 1983. *Enemy Alien.* San Francisco: JAM.

Hirasuna, Delphine. 2005. *The Art of Gaman: Arts and Crafts from the Japanese American Internment Camps 1942–1946.* Berkeley: Ten Speed.

Holborn, Mark. 1978. *The Ocean in the Sand: Japan, from Landscape to Garden.* Boulder: Shambhala.

Hoobler, Dorothy, and Thomas Hoobler. 1996. *The Japanese American Family Album.* New York: Oxford University Press.

Horimoto, Phillip. 1943. "Junior Victory Garden Success." *Mystic,* Amache Junior High, 1.

Horiuchi, Lynn. 2005. "Dislocations and the Relocations: The Built Environments of Japanese American Internment." PhD dissertation, Department of Art History, University of California, Santa Barbara.

Hosokawa, Bill. 2005. *Colorado's Japanese Americans: From 1886 to the Present.* Boulder: University Press of Colorado.

House Beautiful. 1960. "The Smallest Gardens in the World." *House Beautiful* 102 (8): 68–71.

Houston, Jeanne Wakatsuki. 1973. *Farewell to Manzanar: A True Story of Japanese American Experience during and after the World War II Internment.* Edited by James D. Houston. Boston: Houghton Mifflin.

Ichioka, Yuji. 1988. *The Issei: The World of the First Generation Japanese Immigrants, 1885–1924.* New York: Collier Macmillan.

Ikagawa, Toshihiko. 1994. "Residential Gardens in Urban Honolulu, Hawai'i: Neighborhood, Ethnicity, and Ornamental Plants." PhD dissertation, Department of Geography, University of Hawaii, Honolulu.

Inada, Lawson Fusao. 1997. *Drawing the Line: Poems.* Minneapolis: Coffee House Press.

Irvine, Gregory. 2013. *Japonisme and the Rise of the Modern Art Movement: The Arts of the Meiji Period, the Khalili Collection.* London: Thames and Hudson.

Itoh, Teiji. 1973. *Space and Illusion in the Japanese Garden.* Edited by Sōsei Kuzunishi. New York: Weatherhill.

Japanese American Citizens League. 2013. "Power of Words Handbook: A Guide to Language about Japanese Americans in World War II." https://jacl.org/wordpress/wp-content/uploads/2015/08/Power-of-Words-Rev.-Term.-Handbook.pdf.

JCOLD, Japan Commission on Large Dams. 2009. *Dams in Japan: Past, Present, and Future.* Boca Raton, FL: CRC.

Jiler, James. 2006. *Doing Time in the Garden: Life Lessons through Prison Horticulture.* Oakland, CA: New Village.

Jones, John G. 2012. "Analysis of Pollen from Amache Internment Camp, Colorado." In *Archaeological Investigations at the Granada Relocation Center (Amache), National Historic Landmark, Prowers County, Colorado: Report on the 2010 Field Season,* edited by Bonnie J. Clark, David Garrison, and Paul Swader, appendix C. University of Denver, Department of Anthropology.

Jones, John G. 2015. *Analysis of Pollen and Phytoliths from Amache: A Japanese Internment Camp in Colorado.* University of Denver, Department of Anthropology, DU Amache Project Files.

Jones, John G. 2017. *Analysis of Pollen and Phytoliths from Amache, 2016: A Japanese Internment Camp in Colorado.* University of Denver, Department of Anthropology, DU Amache Project Files.

Jones, John G. 2019. *Analysis of Pollen and Phytoliths from Amache, 2018: A Japanese Internment Camp in Colorado.* University of Denver, Department of Anthropology, DU Amache Project Files.

Jones, John G., and Sarah A. Williams. 2015. "Analysis of Pollen Samples from Sediments Collected during the 2012 Amache Field Season." In *Archaeological Investigations at the Granada Relocation Center (Amache), National Historic Landmark, Prowers County, Colorado: Report on the 2012 Field Season,* by Christian Driver and Bonnie J. Clark, appendix B. Prepared for History Colorado, State Historical Fund. University of Denver, Department of Anthropology.

Kamp-Whittaker, April. 2010. "Through the Eyes of a Child: The Archaeology of WWII Japanese American Internment at Amache." MA thesis, Department of Anthropology, University of Denver.

Kamp-Whittaker, April, and Bonnie J. Clark. 2019. "Creating a Community in Confinement: The Development of Neighborhoods in Amache, a World War II Japanese American Internment Camp." In *The Archaeology of Removal in North America,* edited by Terrance Weik, 157–188. Gainesville: University of Florida Press.

Kaneko, Kay Uno, and Edwin Kaneko. 2013. Interview. Edited by Bonnie J. Clark. Notes in possession of author.

Kawana, Koichi. 1977. "Symbolism and Esthetics in the Traditional Japanese Garden." *AABGA Bulletin* (American Association of Botanical Gardens and Arboreta) (April): 33–37.

Kishaba, Lucy, ed. 2003. *Giri: Giving Back, Moving Forward.* Rohnert Park, CA: Sonoma County Japanese American Citizens League.

Kjeldgaard, Enola. 1998. "Impressions of a Japanese Relocation Center: Lest We Forget." Manuscript in possession of author.

Kurano, Hiroo. 2016. "The Special Relevance of Sukiya Architecture for North American Japanese Gardens." *Journal of the North American Japanese Garden Association* (3): 19–24.

Kurisu, Hoichi. 2016. "An Excerpt from 'Japanese Gardens in the Modern World.'" *Journal of the North American Japanese Garden Association* (3): 2–6.

Lange, Dorothea. 2006. *Impounded: Dorothea Lange and the Censored Images of Japanese American Internment.* Edited by Linda Gordon and Gary Y. Okihiro. New York: W. W. Norton.

Law, Lisa. 2005. "Home Cooking: Filipino Women and Topographies of the Senses in Hong Kong." In *Empire of the Senses: The Sensual Culture Reader,* edited by David Howes, 224–241. Oxford: Berg.

Lewis, Charles A. 1994. "People-Plant Relationships—Past and Future." In *The Healing Dimensions of People-Plant Relations: Proceedings of a Research Symposium*, edited by Mark Francis, Pat Lindsey, and Jay Stone Rice, 13–25. Davis: University of California, Davis.

Limerick, Patricia. 1992. "Disorientation and Reorientation: The American Landscape Discovered from the West." *Journal of American History* 79 (3): 1021–1049. doi: 10.2307/2080797.

Lurie, George. 1982. "Return to Amache." *Denver Magazine* (May): 33–38.

Malek, Amina-Aïcha, ed. 2013. *Sourcebook for Garden Archaeology: Methods, Techniques, Interpretations, and Field Examples*. Bern, Switzerland: Peter Lang.

Marín-Spiotta, Erika, and Emily Eggleston. 2012. "Camp Amache Soil Chemistry Report." In *Archaeological Investigations at the Granada Relocation Center (Amache), National Historic Landmark, Prowers County, Colorado: Report on the 2010 Field Season*, by Bonnie J. Clark, David Garrison, and Paul Swader, appendix B. University of Denver, Department of Anthropology.

Matsumoto, Valerie J. 1993. *Farming the Home Place: A Japanese American Community in California, 1919–1982*. Ithaca, NY: Cornell University Press.

McGuire, Randall H., and Robert Paynter, eds. 1991. *The Archaeology of Inequality*. Oxford, UK: Blackwell.

Meskell, Lynn. 2002. "Negative Heritage and Past Mastering in Archaeology." *Anthropological Quarterly* 75 (3): 557–574.

Miller, Naomi F., and Kathryn L. Gleason. 1994. "Fertilizer in the Identification and Analysis of Cultivated Soil." In *The Archaeology of Garden and Field*, edited by Naomi F. Miller and Kathryn L Gleason, 25–43. Philadelphia: University of Pennsylvania Press.

Minkel, J. R. 2007. "Bureau Gave Up Names of Japanese-Americans in WW II." *Scientific American* (March 30).

Morita, E., S. Fukuda, J. Nagano, N. Hamajima, H. Yamamoto, Y. Iwai, T. Nakashima, H. Ohira, and T. Shirakawa. 2007. "Psychological Effects of Forest Environments on Healthy Adults: Shinrin-yoku (Forest-Air Bathing, Walking) as a Possible Method of Stress Reduction." *Public Health* 121 (1): 54–63.

Morse, Edward Sylvester. 1917. *Japan Day by Day, 1877, 1878–79, 1882–83*. Boston: Houghton Mifflin.

Morse, Edward Sylvester. 1961 [1886]. *Japanese Homes and Their Surroundings*. New York: Dover.

Munsterberg, Hugo. 1978. *The Art of Modern Japan: From the Meiji Restoration to the Meiji Centennial, 1868–1968*. New York: Hacker Art Books.

Nagata, Donna K. 1993. *Legacy of Injustice: Exploring the Cross-Generational Impact of the Japanese American Internment*. New York: Plenum.

Nakamaki, Hirochika. 2003. *Japanese Religions at Home and Abroad: Anthropological Perspectives*. London: Routledge Curzon.

Nakano, Mei. 2016. "History of the Sonoma County JACL." http://www.sonoma cojacl.org/About_Us.html.

Ng, Laura. 2014. "Altered Lives, Altered Environments: Creating Home at Manzanar Relocation Center, 1942–1945." MA thesis, Department of Historical Archaeology, University of Massachusetts, Boston.

Nishizaki, Fumiye. 2011. Interview. Edited by DU Amache. University of Denver, Department of Anthropology, DU Amache Project Files.

Noda, Kesa. 1981. *The Yamato Colony, 1906–1960*. Livingston, CA: Livingston-Merced JACL Chapter.

Okihiro, Gary Y., ed. 2013. *Encyclopedia of Japanese American Internment*. Santa Barbara, CA: Greenwood.

Ono, Gary T. 2013. "Jack Muro, the Underground Photographer of Amache." *Discover Nikkei*. http://www.discovernikkei.org/en/journal/2013/5/13/jack-muro/.

Otto, Jennifer. 2009. "Communities Negotiating Preservation: The World War II Internment Camp of Amache." In *Southeast Colorado Heritage Tourism Report*, edited by Rudi Hartmann, 125–139. Denver: Wash Park Media.

Payne, Shenero. 1909. *Tariff Hearings before the Committee: Sixtieth Congress 1908–1909*. Schedule A–N. Washington, DC: Government Printing Office.

Peterson, Whitney. 2018. "Snapshots of Confinement: Memory and Materiality of Japanese Americans' World War II–Era Photo Albums." MA thesis, Department of Anthropology, University of Denver.

The Pulse. 1943. "Amache in Retrospective." Supplement to the *Granada Pioneer* (May), 11–12.

Raggett, Jill. 2018. "Japanese Gardens in the UK and the Japanese Garden Society." *Journal of the North American Japanese Garden Association* (5): 33–35.

Reader, Ian. 1993. *Japanese Religions: Past and Present*. Edited by Esben Andreasen and Finn Stefánsson. Honolulu: University of Hawaii Press.

Rheannon, Francesca. 2008. Interview with Terry Tempest Williams. *Writer's Voice*. http://www.writersvoice.net/2008/10/terry-tempest-williams-mosaic/.

Riggs, Erin Paige. 2013. "The Domoto Diaspore: An Investigation of One Family's Experience of and Influence within American Landscapes from 1882 through Today." Senior honors thesis, Department of Anthropology, University of California, Berkeley.

Roath, L. Roy, Rachel Ridenour, Bob Wesley, and Zachary Holmes. 2008. "Vegetation Inventory, Sand Creek Massacre National Historic Site: A Report for the Southern Plains Network." Fort Collins: US Department of the Interior, National Park Service and Natural Resource Program Center, Colorado State University. https://www.nps.gov/sand/learn/nature/upload/Veg-inventory_Roath.pdf.

Robinson, Greg. 2010. *A Tragedy of Democracy: Japanese Confinement in North America*. New York: Columbia University Press.

Sakaguchi, Mac. 1943. "Editorial: Gardens." *Mystic*, Amache Junior High, June 15, 2.

Sako, Suyeo. 1943a. "Unsung Heroes and Heroines." *Granada Pioneer*, November 17.

Sako, Suyeo. 1943b. "Thumbnail Sketches." *Granada Pioneer*, May 15.

Sako, Suyeo. 1943c. "Thumbnail Sketches." *Granada Pioneer*, September 1, 4.

Salzer, Kenneth E. 1942. "Introduction." *Salzer Seed Company Catalog*, January, 1.

Sasaki, Mizue. 2006. "Perspectives of Language: Cultural Differences and Universality in Japanese." In *Cultural Diversity and Transversal Values: East-West Dialogue on Spiritual and Secular Dynamics*, edited by Samantha Wauchope, 119–126. Paris: UNESCO.

Schrager, Adam. 2008. *The Principled Politician: The Ralph Carr Story*. Golden, CO: Fulcrum.

Schroeder, Fred E.H. 1993. *Front Yard America: The Evolution and Meanings of a Vernacular Domestic Landscape*. Bowling Green, OH: Bowling Green State Popular Press.

Seffense, Courtney. 2019. *Amache Soil Chemistry Report: 2016 Field Season*. University of Denver, Department of Anthropology, DU Amache Project Files.

Seki, Kiyohide. 1971. "The Circle of On, Giri, and Ninjo: Sociologist's Point of View." *Annual Reports on Cultural Science* 19 (2): 99–114.

Seki, Sankyaku, ed. 2007. *Gardeners' Pioneer Story: As Preserved in Senryu Poems Written by Nikkei Gardeners*. Los Angeles: Southern California Gardeners' Federation.

Sekikawa, Helen Yagi. 2013. Interview. Edited by Bonnie J. Clark. University of Denver, Department of Anthropology, DU Amache Project Files.

Shanks, Michael, and Randall H. McGuire. 1996. "The Craft of Archaeology." *American Antiquity* 61 (1): 75–88.

Sharps, J. A. 1976. "Geologic Map of the Lamar Quadrangle, Colorado and Kansas." *US Geological Survey*. http://ngmdb.usgs.gov/Prodesc/proddesc_9832.htm.

Shew, Dana Ogo. 2010. "Feminine Identity Confined: The Archaeology of Japanese Women at Amache, a WWII Internment Camp." MA thesis, Department of Anthropology, University of Denver.

Shigekuni, Thomas. 2011. Interview. Edited by Bonnie J. Clark and David Garrison. University of Denver, Department of Anthropology, DU Amache Project Files.

Simmons, Thomas H., and R. Laurie Simmons. 1993. "Granada Relocation Center, National Register of Historic Places Nomination Form." Denver: Front Range Research Associates, Inc.

Simmons, Thomas H., and R. Laurie Simmons. 2004. "Granada Relocation Center, National Historic Landmark Nomination Form." Form Prepared for the National Park Service. Denver: Front Range Research Associates, Inc.

Singleton, Theresa A., ed. 1999. *"I, Too, Am America": Archaeological Studies of African-American Life*. Charlottesville: University Press of Virginia.

Skiles, Stephanie, and Bonnie J. Clark. 2010. "When the Foreign Is Not Exotic: Ceramics at Colorado's WWII Japanese Internment Camp." In *Trade and Exchange: Archaeological Studies from History and Prehistory*, edited by Carolyn Dillian and Carolyn White, 179–192. New York: Springer.

Slaughter, Michelle A. 2006. "An Archaeological and Ethnographic Examination of the Presence, Acquisition, and Consumption of Sake at Camp Amache, a World War II Japanese Internment Camp." MA thesis, Department of Anthropology, University of Colorado at Denver.

Slawson, David A. 1987. "Illustrations for Designing Mountain, Water, and Hillside Field Landscapes." In *Secret Teachings in the Art of Japanese Gardens: Design Principles, Aesthetic Values*, edited by David A. Slawson, 142–173. Tokyo: Kodansha International.

Smith, Marian L. 2002. "Race, Nationality, and Reality: INS Administration of Racial Provisions in US Immigration and Nationality Law since 1898." Prologue Magazine 34 (2). https://www.archives.gov/publications/prologue/2002/summer/immigration-law-1.html.

Smith, Thomas C. 1977. *Nakahara: Family Farming and Population in a Japanese Village, 1717–1830.* Edited by Robert T. Lundy. Stanford, CA: Stanford University Press.

Sobisha. 1990. *Daisen-in: Including All the Gardens and Tea Houses of Daitoku-ji.* Kyoto: Daisen-in.

Starke, Zachary. 2015. "Wrestling with Tradition: Japanese Activities at Amache, a World War II Incarceration Facility." MA thesis, Department of Anthropology, University of Denver.

Swader, Paul. 2015. "An Analysis of Modified Material Culture from Amache: Investigating the Landscape of Japanese American Internment." MA thesis, Department of Anthropology, University of Denver.

Tagsold, Christian. 2017. *Spaces in Translation: Japanese Gardens and the West.* Philadelphia: University of Pennsylvania Press.

Takei, Jirō, and Marc P. Keane. 2001. *Sakuteiki, Visions of the Japanese Garden: A Modern Translation of Japan's Gardening Classic.* Boston: Tuttle.

Tamura, Anna. 2004. "Gardens Below the Watchtower: Gardens and Meaning in World War II Japanese American Incarceration Camps." *Landscape Journal* 23: 1–21.

Tanaka, Alice Fukuda. 2011. Interview with DU Amache. Edited by Bonnie J. Clark, Christian Driver, and David Garrison. University of Denver, Department of Anthropology, DU Amache Project Files.

Tonai, Minoru. 2011. Interview. Edited by Bonnie J. Clark, Christian Driver, and David Garrison. University of Denver, Department of Anthropology, DU Amache Project Files.

Toulouse, Julian Harrison. 2001. *Bottle Makers and Their Marks.* Caldwell, NJ: Blackburn.

Trelstad, Brian. 1997. "Little Machines in Their Gardens: A History of School Gardens in America, 1891–1920." *Landscape Journal* 16 (2): 161–173.

Tsuchida, Motoko. 1998. "A History of Japanese Emigration from the 1860s to the 1990s." In *Temporary Workers or Future Citizens?* edited by Myron Weiner and Tadashi Hanami, 77–119. London: Palgrave Macmillan.

Tsukashima, Ronald. 2000. "Politics of Maintenance Gardening and the Formation of the Southern California Gardeners' Federation." In *Greenmakers: Japanese American Gardeners in Southern California*, edited by Naomi Hirahara, 66–93. Los Angeles: Southern California Gardeners' Federation.

Uchida, Yoshiko. 1982. *Desert Exile: The Uprooting of a Japanese American Family*. Seattle: University of Washington Press.

Uchima, Ansho Mas, and Minoru Shinmoto. 2010. *Seinan, Southwest Los Angeles: Stories and Experiences from Residents of Japanese Ancestry*. Edited by Raymond M. Uyemura. Fullerton: Nikkei Writers Guild Division of Japanese American Living Legacy, California State University.

Ulrich, Roger S. 1984. "View through a Window May Influence Recovery from Surgery." *Science* 224: 420–421.

Ulrich, Roger S. 1999. "Effects of Gardens on Health Outcomes: Theory and Research." In *Healing Gardens: Therapeutic Benefits and Design Recommendations*, edited by Clare Cooper Marcus and Marni Barnes, 27–86. New York: John Wiley and Sons.

Unknown. 1944. "Rhythm Show Program." Japanese Americans in World War II Collection, Fresno State University, Fresno, CA.

US Bureau of the Census. 1940. *Population Schedules of the Sixteenth Census*. Accessed through Ancestry.com.

US Selective Service System. 1912. Draft registration card, Zenkishi Sairyo. Accessed through Ancestry.com.

US Selective Service System. 1918. Draft registration card, Kahichi Yokoi. Accessed through Ancestry.com.

US Selective Service System. 1942. Draft registration card, Tsuneo Shigekuni. Accessed through Ancestry.com.

Viellard-Baron, Michel. 2007. "Religious and Lay Rituals in Japanese Gardens during the Heian Period (784–1185)." In *Sacred Gardens and Landscapes: Ritual and Agency*, edited by Michel Conan, 57–66. Washington, DC: Dumbarton Oaks Research Library and Collection. Distributed by Harvard University Press.

Voon, Claire. 2017. "The Japanese American Architect Who Was a Disciple of Frank Lloyd Wright." *Hyperallergic* (November 10). https://hyperallergic.com/392963/kaneji-domoto-frank-lloyd-wright-usonia/.

Wall, Diana DiZerega. 1991. "Sacred Dinners and Secular Teas: Constructing Domesticity in Mid-Nineteenth-Century New York." *Historical Archaeology* 25 (4): 69–81.

Wann, David. 2003. *The Zen of Gardening in the High and Arid West: Tips, Tools, and Techniques*. Golden, CO: Fulcrum.

Warner, Sam Bass, Jr. 1994. "The Periodic Rediscoveries of Restorative Gardens: 1100 to the Present." In *The Healing Dimensions of People-Plant Relations: Proceedings of a Research Symposium*, edited by Mark Francis, Pat Lindsey, and Jay Stone Rice, 5–12. Davis: University of California, Davis.

Weglyn, Michi. 1996. *Years of Infamy: The Untold Story of America's Concentration Camps.* Updated ed. Seattle: University of Washington Press.

Wei, William. 2016. *Asians in Colorado: A History of Persecution and Perseverance in the Centennial State.* Scott and Laurie Oki Series in Asian American Studies. Seattle: University of Washington Press.

Wilkie, Laurie A. 2006. "Documentary Archaeology." In *The Cambridge Companion to Historical Archaeology,* edited by Dan Hicks and Mary C. Beaudry, 13–33. Cambridge: University of Cambridge Press.

WRA, War Relocation Authority. 1943a. *The Problem Concerning Tenant Disposition.* Housing Department of the WRA. NARA, Records Group 210, FILM B 3062, Reel 47, Folder 37. National Archives, Washington, DC.

WRA, War Relocation Authority. 1943b. *Report on Attitudes at Amache.* NARA, Records Group 210, FILM B 3062, Reel 47, Folder 37. National Archives, Washington, DC.

WRA, War Relocation Authority. 1945. *Granada Project Chronological History.* Physical copy in the DU Amache Project Files. National Archives, Washington, DC.

WRA, War Relocation Authority. 1946. *Final Accountability Rosters of Evacuees, 1944–46, Granada Relocation Center.* Accessed through Ancestry.com.

WRA, War Relocation Authority. n.d. *Parent-School Relations Program.* NARA, Records Group 210, FILM B 3062, Reel 45, Folder 17. National Archives, Washington, DC.

Yamin, Rebecca, and Karen Bescherer Metheny, eds. 1996. *Landscape Archaeology: Reading and Interpreting the American Historical Landscape.* Knoxville: University of Tennessee Press.

Zimmerman, Larry J., and Jessica Welch. 2011. "Displaced and Barely Visible: Archaeology and the Material Culture of Homelessness." *Historical Archaeology* 45 (1): 67–85.

Index